MY LIFE IN CHRIST

by Eustace Mullins

DEDICATION –
To Nil'. II. L. HUNT,
a truly Christian gentleman

EUSTACE CLARENCE MULLINS
(1923-2010)

My life in Christ

1968

MY LIFE IN CHRIST is not an apologia pro vita sua, but an indictment, it is the indictment of Satan's Empire on earth. EUSTACE MULLINS, 1968

Published by
OMNIA VERITAS LTD

www.omnia-veritas.com

ABOUT THE AUTHOR 9
CHAPTER ONE 11
   LIVING IN CHRIST 11
   TRANSCENDENCE 11
   CHRIST'S KINGDOM 12
   BECOMING WORTHY OF CHRIST 13
   NOTHING HAS CHANGED 13
   THE APOSTLES 14
   FOLLOWING CHRIST 15
   LOYALTY 16
   COMMUNISM 17
   GREED 20
   WORK 22
   RITUAL WORSHIP 25
   THE IGNORAMUS 27
   THE TRUE KNIGHT OF CHRIST 31
   CRIPPLED GENTILES 33
   ACKNOWLEDGING CHRIST 34
   THE UNATTAINABLE CHRIST 34
   RESURRECTION 37
   HUMILITY 38
   ANIMATION 40
   DIVINE PROTECTION 41
   DRUGS 44
   DENYING CHRIST 48
   THE HARMONY OF THE SPHERES 50
   YOUTH 53
   BECOMING AN ADULT 58
   OUR MISSION 60
   LOVE 61
   ATMOSPHERE 63
   WHY CHRIST? 64
   THE BIRTH OF CHRIST 67
   THE SUFFERING OF CHRIST 69
   THE SELF 72

CHAPTER TWO 74
   SATAN'S EMPIRE 74

INTELLIGENT	74
CRIPPLES	77
GET RID OF THE CIA AND THE FBI	78
RUIN OF THE CIA	78
COMMUNIST PROPAGANDA AGENCY	79
BECOMES CIA	80
GENTILE FRONT	81
REVOLUTION IN LATIN AMERICA	82
MASQUERADE AS PRIESTS	83
BATISTA	84
COUNTER-REVOLUTION	84
HUNGARIAN ATROCITY	86
CIA PERSONNEL	87
ORIGIN OF THE FBI	88
SURVIVOR	88
TILE "ITALIAN" MAFIA	89
HATES NEGROES	90
HOOVER SWALLOWS HIS PRIDE	92
FBI REIGN OF TERROR	93
REMODELING THE SYNAGOGUES	93
HOOVER A FRONT MAN	94
THE KENNEDY MYTH	95
THE GREAT AMERICAN PHONIES	96
THE STALIN-TROTSKY IMPASSE	97
GARRISON	101
THE KATZENBACISTS	102
SLAVES	102
OPEN WAR	105
WHITE REPRESSION	107
EQUAL JUSTICE UNDER LAW	107
THE "BLACK" REVOLUTION IN AMERICA	108
CHAPTER THREE	**110**
HOW I CAME TO CHRIST	110
A BEGINNING	111
FIRST BLOOD	114
A BUSY LIFE	116
I COME TO MCCARTHY'S AID	116
THE COHN AND SCHINE CIRCUS	117
THE NEW YORK YEARS	118
CHICAGO YEARS	119

DIFFICULT YEARS	122
SERENITY	122
LIVING IN CHRIST	123
REAL LIFE	125
THE MURDER OF MY FATHER	127
MURDER, INC.	129
THE ASSASSIN'S BLOW	131
ATTEMPTS AGAINST MY LIFE	132
AT HOME IN VIRGINIA	133
THE CRIME AGAINST MY SISTER	134
THE ARMY OF CHRIST	136
CHRIST POWER	137
EDUCATION IN CHRIST	139
OTHER WORK BY EUSTACE MULLINS	**142**

Eustace Mullins

About the author

In forty years of dedicated investigative research, **Eustace Mullins** has drawn considerable return fire. He was kept under daily surveillance by agents of the FBI for thirty-two years; no charges were ever placed against him. He is the only person ever fired from the staff of the Library of Congress for political reasons. He is the only writer who has had a book burned in Europe since 1945.

After serving thirty-eight months in the U. S. Army Air Force during World War II, **Eustace Mullins** was educated at Washington and Lee University, Ohio State University, University of North Dakota, and New York University. He later studied art at the Escuela des Bellas Artes, San Miguel de Allende, Mexico, and the Institute of Contemporary Arts, Washington, D.C.

While studying in Washington, he was asked to go to St. Elizabeth's Hospital to talk to the nation's most famous political prisoner, Ezra Pound. The outstanding literary figure of the twentieth century, Pound had seen three of his pupils awarded the Nobel Prize, while it was denied to him because of his pronouncements as a native American patriot. Not only did **Eustace Mullins** become his most active protege, he is the only person who keeps Ezra Pound's name alive today, through the work of the Ezra Pound Institute of Civilization, which was founded shortly after the poet's death in Venice.

Eustace Mullins (1923-2010) is considered one of the greatest political historians of the 20th Century.

CHAPTER ONE

LIVING IN CHRIST

THIS is the story of my life in Christ. Now, what does living in Christ mean? It means that one is FOR Christ, that one not only accepts Him, but that one lives in Him. Living in Christ has little relationship to the more commonly accepted situation of living as a Christian, or living a Christian life. Living AS a Christian means that one has accepted the tokens of Christianity, that one agrees in the divinity of Christ, that one is a member of a Christian congregation, in a largely Christian community, in a Christian nation. Thus, one can lead a Christian life without knowing Christ and without changing one's existence in the slightest degree.

TRANSCENDENCE

If a person leads a Christian life, and it does not transform one's existence, then one can be sure that he does not KNOW Christ. Knowing Christ is the only manner in which one can go beyond oneself, and the only manner in which one can go beyond one's world. In knowing Christ, one is immediately lifted out of the mechanical life of the human existence, one transcends the common existence. One is no longer a human machine, leading a hopeless, mechanical life, repeating the same meaningless motions like a robot throughout the years of one's earthly existence. What was Christ's ad-monition? "Take up the Cross, and follow Me." But, in explication of this admonition, the New Testament contains many significant references to the condition of sleep, and Christ's exhortations to mankind to awaken. Now, what does this mean? It means that Christ did not wish to be followed by robots and sleepwalkers, He desired man to awaken, and to attain the full use of his earthly powers. Not only are mechanical men of no use to Christ, but they are quite dangerous, they present endless difficulties in the establishment of Christ's Kingdom on earth.

CHRIST'S KINGDOM

Throughout history, we have come to think of kingdoms as something bad, as countries in which the people toil for the profit of a king. This is what earthly kingdoms become, because kings are men, and men have their limitations. But the Kingdom of Christ on earth is something more than this, and when He said, "My Kingdom is not of this world," He meant that His Kingdom could not be a kingdom like other kingdoms of this world, in which men lead toilsome, meaningless lives. Christ's Kingdom is a Kingdom in which men transcend themselves and their world. Only then are they worthy of

Christ; only then do they know Christ.

BECOMING WORTHY OF CHRIST

How does one come to know Christ, how does one awaken, how does one become worthy of Christ? In order to awaken, one opens one's eyes, and this means that one can no longer shut one's eyes to the conditions of this world. We live in a world in which evil has become paramount, in which evil is the sole means of government, in which evil is leading all men to disaster. But we endure this world by pretending that evil is either non-existent or unimportant. As long as we pretend this, we cannot know Christ. Once we acknowledge that our world is a world of evil, we have made the first step towards knowing Christ. And when we begin to combat that evil, we begin to live in Christ. But, protests the sceptic, Christ came down to earth two thousand years ago to prevail against evil. If He could not prevail, how can man be expected to?

NOTHING HAS CHANGED

Of course, nothing has changed since Christ appeared on earth two thousand years ago. The Elders of Zion who ordered His physical execution are still ordering the massacres of thousands of Christians all over the world.

The Devil is still in the saddle, spreading war and destruction over the world. Christ did not prevail, because Christ was not meant to prevail. This is the great fallacy which misleads so many Christians today.

I can sit back and do nothing, because Christ will do it all. Christ did not prevail, because His mission was to show man the Way. I am the Way, the Truth and the Light. What meaning would our existence have, if we did not take up the struggle against evil? It would have, unfortunately, just the meaning which most men's lives have today, that is, it would have no meaning at all. A meaningless existence — is that Christ's punishment for those of us who do not take up the fight? NO, it is not His punishment, because Christ does not punish anyone. We punish ourselves for our failure to take up the fight, because we sentence ourselves to a meaningless existence, an existence in which we do not know Christ.

THE APOSTLES

Take up the Cross and follow Me. This is the lesson which illuminates the lives of the Apostles. Not only are the Apostles of Christ living examples of how one should set about knowing Christ, and following Him, but they are also of great symbolic importance, for they symbolize the Twelve Over souls, the Twelve Masters who inform all of man's life on earth. Christ often communicates with us through one of the Apostles, the still, small voice which orders or persuades us to do something, perhaps against our will, and which has great effect on our lives. One of the great characteristics of awakening in Christ is that one becomes more aware of His Will, just as one of the great characteristics of living surrounded by evil on this earth is that one becomes deaf to Christ's Will, one is unable to receive His messages.

FOLLOWING CHRIST

One of the true characteristics of Christian civilization is a periodic awakening of many men, who devote themselves to Christ. The first example of this was the Apostles. There have been many subsequent ones, such as the Knight Hospitallers, who became True Knights of Christ. This means that they lived their lives in absolute dedication to the principles of Christ, that they were Knights, militant, chivalrous, and faithful. They carried on their lives in the great traditions of Christian civilization, following unshakable principles of honour, and living in pride, because, far from being a vice, pride becomes a virtue when one lives in Christ. Pride among those who live materialistic lives is not a. virtue, because they are proud of their fine clothes, their beautiful homes and their protruding bellies. But when one lives in Christ, one is proud of one's courage, one's honour, and one's deeds for Christ. Because evil is everywhere on earth, there are always great crusades awaiting the spirit of those who are willing to fight for Christ. In the world of today, no man can be proud of what he is. He can only be proud of what he may become, when he devotes his life to Christ.

LOYALTY

One of the outstanding characteristics of the Knight Hospitallers was their loyalty. One who lives in Christ is loyal to one's family and one's country. Christ said, Render unto Caesar the things that are Caesar's. This means that we can give to a government the material things that government requires, such as taxes, and we can give loyalty to that government when that government is a Christian one. Now, one of the great features of those who are against Christ is their disloyalty, not merely disloyalty to Christ, but disloyalty to their employers, to their countries and to every institution of Christian civilization. Today we find that disloyalty and subversion are everywhere, because they are manifestations of evil. Now, we frequently read about and hear of church leaders who advocate disloyalty, who preach subversion, and whose only apparent mission in life is to see all of the institutions of Christian civilization overthrown and destroyed. Yet these are people who have risen to high positions in Christian life. But how have they risen to these positions? Did you choose them? Of course not. They rose to these high positions precisely because they were subversives, because other traitors aided them in attaining these high positions, from which they hope to wreck all Christian institutions. Is it so easy, then, to use Christ to destroy Christ? It is not easy at all. We must remember that the rise of these church leaders to important positions is the result of many years of arduous conspiracies, planning, and hard work on the part of the subversives. This also illustrates the danger of allowing Christian churches and Christian nations to be led by men who do not know Christ, because some of these are mechanical men, men who are asleep at the switch, men who do not consciously do the evil that they do because they are not conscious of anything, they are unconscious instruments of evil.

COMMUNISM

What is the chief characteristic of Communism? Ali, says modern man, the chief characteristic of Communism is the abolition of private property. But this is not the important thing about Communism. Communism means living in hatred of Jesus Christ. The Jew, Karl Marx, who is known as the Father of Communism, was brought up by his family to hate Jesus Christ, and this remains the principal characteristic of Communism. The hatred of Christ which Karl Marx imbibed at his father's knee informs every Communist institution. Communism also means the subversion and destruction of Christian civilization. Everyone who lives in a Christian country and follows Communist principles is a traitor. Thus, we know in America thousands of these traitors who occupy important positions in church leadership, education, and government offices. Everyday we read about new instances of treason. This widespread sedition occurs because Americans do not know Christ. Many of these traitors claim to be Christians. Often we find that they have been laying down national policies for important denominations of Christian churches. But you did not appoint these "Christian" leaders. They rose to power because of their membership in secret Communist cell groups which have operated underground in this country for more than fifty years. In reviewing their careers, you discover that everything that they have done and everything that they have said throughout their careers has been done according to the principles of Communism and in hatred of Jesus Christ. Then you, in accepting these church leaders, are a mechanical man, a robot, unable to know Christ.

Living in Christ demands that you use your mind, exercise your intelligence. Anyone who tries to stupefy you, to prevent you from developing your mind, or argues against your thinking for yourself, does not know Christ. Christ has no secrets, Christ is not trying to keep anything from you. Living in Christ means that you become a philosopher, you live by a philosophy of life. Now, what does philosophy mean? It comes from two Greek words. *phil,* and *sophia,* meaning, the love of wisdom, or the pursuit of wisdom. Webster's Dictionary gives a further definition, which it labels as Archaic, or no longer applicable to the modern world. This archaic definition of philosophy is "the study of natural phenomena". Now, why did the study of natural phenomena. become an archaic meaning of philosophy? Why was philosophy removed from man's knowledge of the natural world, and sentenced to wither in the stuffy classrooms of universities? Obviously, because some men turned the study of philosophy away from God's world, Philosophy reached its greatest heights nearly two thousand years ago, when such philosophers as Aristotle observed everything in nature, studied and wrote about God's world. But then the Jews came out of their ghettoes, carrying their Books of the Talmud, and they became our new philosophers. Ignoring all of God's world about them, they argue endlessly over the turn of a phrase and the meaning of one word, and since they do not know Christ, the Light of the World, for them everything is in darkness. As a result, philosophy, as given to us by Jews, has lost all relevance to the world we live in. We find that nearly all books about philosophy today follow Talmudic principles, argue semantics, and ignore the living world. They are written by Jewish "scholars", published by Jewish publishing houses, and reviewed by Jewish professors. Philosophy will play a living role again only then it is allowed to live, when it returns to its "archaic" definition of "the study of natural phenomena."

We also should understand that "natural phenomena" are not limited to the rising and setting of the sun. Mystical experiences are also natural phenomena, as there is nothing "unnatural" in God's world. We try to restrict ourselves to what is near and familiar, because we are afraid, but when we come to know Christ, we no longer have this fear, and we can venture forth to experience much more of God's universe.

GREED

One of the problems of mankind is the problem of greed, of those who must have more than their share. We must realize that all greed stems from fear and insecurity, the fear of not having enough. When one begins to know Christ, this sort of fear and insecurity disappears forever, because one knows that one lives in divine harmony, and one will be provided for in God's world. This does not mean that one is absolved from all future effort, or that one will be fed miraculously from Heaven, but it does mean that one will not know want.

The concept of manna from Heaven is a typically Jewish one, in that this people, who were unable to provide for themselves through useful labour, attempted to make God liable for their continuing a parasitic existence by miraculously delivering them food from Heaven. Parasitism and materialism are the two greatest instruments of evil in the modern world, the parasitism of the Jews and the materialism of the Communists. The Jews expect to be fed without effort on their part; the Communists believe that the human organism is a machine, and that everything can be reduced to the needs of feeding, clothing and sheltering this machine according to the technology of other machines.

Both parasitism and materialism are complete misconceptions of man's existence in God's world. One cannot live without effort; neither can one live as a machine. The idea that stoking the human machine is the end-all of earthly existence is a Communist idea, whether the believer is a factory owner in New England, a banker in France, or a commissar in Russia, because this is materialism. It is also blind stupidity.

This does not mean that Christ is a non-materialist, or an anti-materialist. He appeared on earth in a material form, He materialized. But materialism is only a point of departure, it is not the goal. Anyone who makes materialism his goal cannot know Christ. Now, does this mean that one should take vows of poverty, foreswear comfort, wear animal skins and live in a cave? Certainly not. Christ went out into the world as He found it. One can know Christ and live in the world, only if one is not overcome by the world. One can live as materially as one wishes, working and storing up whatever one decides is worth having, IF one does not make this the final goal. The goal is to know Christ.

Now, knowing Christ is not an "escape" from materialism, nor is it an escape from the world. Christ is not an escape from anything, for we cannot escape anything in a material existence. Life is a prison in which all of us are locked. The idea of escape is endemic in everything in modern life, because we have come to know that we ARE in prison. What we do not realize, when we do not know Christ, is that the prison doors are not locked, that we can open them and go out, that Christ is the Way.

We remain in prison only because we are not worthy of being free, we do not really wish to be free. This is because we are prisoners of our mechanical concept of life, and all of our material goals are the doors which shut us in our prison. There are no jailers, there are no locked doors, but everything in modern life is a jailer, and everything in life today fastens onto our minds the concept of locked doors. It is these concepts which prevent us from reaching out and pushing open the doors, of going forth to live in Christ.

WORK

There has probably been more nonsense written about work than any other aspect of man's existence. We know the "dignity of work" thesis, a theory always propounded by those who have never done a day of manual labor in their lives. This theory is always given to us by pink palmed bankers and lawyers, who live on the fruits of our labor. This writer began a life of hard work at the age of eleven, and has worked ever since, but he has never written a word in praise of "the dignity of labour".

Work is a condition of man's existence, it is a mechanical

aspect, akin to breathing, and to providing food and water for the human organism. Now, these are physical necessities; there is nothing ennobling per se about taking a deep breath or putting in a hard day's work. We do these things because we have to, because they are a part of this existence, but we should know that this is a step towards a higher existence, towards knowing Christ_ Many workers do not realize this, they work but they look no further. But those who do go on have backgrounds of hard work. Christ did manual labour as a carpenter before going forth on His earthly mission. And there are examples today. The Washington seeress Jeanne Dixon frequently reminds people that she put in twenty-five years of hard work before she could afford time for meditation. The late Edgar Cayce worked as a photographer. Work remains an oppressive reality for many of us because we do not look beyond. My friend, the late Edith Hamilton, said, "It is not hard work which is dreary, but superficial work." Most of the work that we do is superficial, it has little meaning except as part of a mechanical existence, but we must look beyond this work, and prepare ourselves for living in Christ.

Because we are oppressed by work, we like to believe that other people are not, that wealthy people lead a carefree existence. We want to believe that Michelangelo carved out his sculptures in a few easy gestures, that Rembrandt painted his works and Beethoven wrote his symphonies in some offhand manner, without continuous and dedicated effort. But the true artist is one who has learned to work, who has succeeded in directing himself to his goal.

Another school of thought claims that it is work which gives depth and meaning to our lives. This theory is also a favourite one among those people who live off of the work of others, who like to hire people to work long hours at low rates of pay. Now, work is not going to be the ultimate meaning of your life, whether it is simple manual labour or whether it is some more consecrated activity such as helping retarded children or living in the cloisters. Only Christ can give meaning to your life.

Unless you are among a small minority, you are going to have to work, and you should do the best work of which you are capable, just as you should eat sensibly and obey other aspects of mechanical existence. As we have said, work is a condition of human existence, but it is not the goal. This is why retired people find a great emptiness in their lives, because they have allowed their work to dwarf the metaphysical realities of life, they have not prepared themselves for a life beyond work.

For many of us, work is a drug with which we deaden ourselves, and reduce our sensibilities. It is too easy to throw oneself into a job, to shut out everything but one's work, it is like taking a drug. One must realize that the human body is a machine, that the modern technology is a machine. Either we master the machine, or the machine masters us. We are the masters if we look beyond the machine, if we know Christ. But if we accept the machine's values, and live by them, then the machine is victorious.

RITUAL WORSHIP

One of the problems of organized religion, or ritual worship, is that it becomes mechanical, and loses sight of the purpose which originally informed it Thus, Gibbon remarked, in *The Decline and Fall of the Roman Empire:* "The various modes of worship which prevailed in the true, by the philosopher as equally false, and by the magistrate as equally useful." This is strikingly true of the present day, when ecumenism has taught us that all religions are equally tree, while the philosophers ridicule them as equally false, and the judiciary considers them equally useful in maintaining public order.

Now, these are mechanical values, and, if mechanical values are that we ask from religion, then mechanical values are all that we will receive. Why does a spiritual obsession become a mechanical one? Because man approaches everything from a fundamentally utilitarian viewpoint, and even spiritual matters are not exempt from being reduced to mechanical modes. But mechanical modes of worship cannot take us beyond a mechanical world, and if they had originally a more powerful result, such as control of matter through levitation, and other results which would be considered 'miracles" today, then those powers are no longer apparent, Meaningful religious experience is a happening, a mystical achievement, which cannot be attained through purely mechanical means. As a mystical achievement, it is largely restricted to individual experience, although some religious experiences may appear in a mass form.

When people complain that their religion does nothing for them, or that they can see no results from their practices of religion, they are not really complaining about their religion, they are complaining about themselves. They are not giving anything to religion, even though they may be giving time, or money, or emotional support, but they are not giving themselves.

Now, if religion does not add meaning to your life, then you have no religion, whatever faith you may profess. And if you have no religion, you may be called an atheist, although many so-called atheists are more involved, and more concerned with religion than many of the supposedly devout. The reason for this paradox is that many atheists express an active interest in religion, but refuse to accept the established gods of their neighbours. The atheist questions these gods because he does not believe that they are true, and in so doing, he opens the way for a future acceptance of Christ, for many have come to Him by denying Him, not the least of whom was Saul of Tarsus.

THE IGNORAMUS

There is a popular misconception that to be ignorant means that one is stupid. Now, the ignoramus may or may not be stupid, but the primary meaning of ignoramus is one who ignores, one who blinds oneself to the Mission of Christ and the splendour of God's universe. It is these ignoramuses whom one finds everywhere in positions of leadership today, these people who ignore Christ are prominent in business, in government, in education, and in the churches. In the main, they are persons who have won success by carrying out some minor repetitive action ad infinitum, and who, because they know how to move one tiny cog in such a way that the machine functions, are hailed everywhere as brilliant and original geniuses. But they have mastered this cog only because they have trained themselves to ignore everything else, including Christ.

Now, why should we allow these ignorant machines, or human beings who have willingly converted themselves into machines, to think for us and to tell us what to think? When we accept this state of affairs, we become more ignorant than the ignoramuses at the top, because we are ignoring the fact that these machines are ignoring Christ. This is truly a situation of the blind leading the blind. We cannot escape the fact that the problem of the ignoranti overshadows everything in modern life. It explains why everything in modern life is fantastic, cheap, and vicious, because the ignoranti are fantastic, cheap, and vicious. That is why we must consider before everything else, the problem of "being ignorant", of ignoring Christ.

By ignoring Christ, the ignoranti cripple themselves, and it is these cripples who now exercise power over us. Why is this? In order to understand this we must understand that we live in a pathological world, a world in which people are shaped and moulded by principles of evil, rather than by principles of good. Instead of being shaped in the mold of Christ, people are pressed into the warped moulds of the Devil. What good transpires comes accidentally, as a by-product of the actions of evil, Thus, a war precipitated by Satan in which deluded and crazed men massacre each other fills hospitals with victims who are torn and mashed into every possible condition, and by studying these victims, doctors make great progress. Modern medicine stems largely from the mass slaughters of World War I. And this is the pathological principle, in which evil is the determining factor in everything which occurs. We cannot begin to understand our condition until we understand that we are surrounded by evil, that evil is the major influence in everything which happens to us and which goes on in the modern world. Look at America!

America and the rest of the world are poised on the brink of the abyss. Laws are written by traitors and administered by criminals. Decent people do not have a chance of obtaining justice in the courts, because many of the judges are the most vicious criminals in America, The scum rises to the top in every walk of life, in the well-paid levels of government, education and entertainment. We are surrounded by filth, noise, and the ravings of degenerate minds, while we sit on a huge stockpile of atomic bombs, enough to blow the world to bits a dozen times. What is the answer? There is no answer, because there is no question. There has never been any question as to the correct manner in which man must live. But, because man's knowledge of himself has been perverted by the polluted and diseased atmosphere in which he lives, he has been given a second chance. That second chance is Jesus Christ. If man had been true to himself, Christ would not have had to embark upon this mission. In the darkness which engulfs us, the radiance of Jesus Christ illuminates everything and restores to us our knowledge of ourselves.

Jesus Christ offers health to a sick humanity, because of God's dismay at the tragic fate which threatens 'part of His universe., Humanity has become a bitter gall, which sours the Garden of Eden which God created here. In all this, we must remember that God has never been a difficult taskmaster. He has never asked anything from us which we cannot easily give. Also, He has provided us in this world with everything which we need. There is a cure in nature for every possible human ailment, because ours is a natural world. He has provided food for every hunger, and in Jesus Christ, hope for all who despair. Despite this providence of Heaven, humanity has become prey to doubts and fears, all of which are sown by Satan, and under the spur of these doubts, man commits atrocities against himself and against all of nature.

A fetid cloud of evil engulfs us, and the radiance of Jesus Christ is the only force which can dispel it. Yet He cannot do this unless we ask it of Him, unless we seek Him and pledge ourselves to His Will. In these times of peril, many people are aware of the danger. They are trying to fight it, to protect themselves and their families, by simple, half-hearted and futile protests against crime, against Communism, against the Satanic government of America and of the world. Their efforts come to no avail. Why is this? We see sincere people risking their property and their lives to fight Communism, to expose criminals, to combat poverty and disease. Many of them lose everything, but no constructive results can be seen. Why is this? These well-meaning people only see one aspect of evil at a time. They are aroused by the evil aspect of Communism, by the evil aspect of crime, but to strike out against only one aspect of evil is to waste one's efforts. We can prevail against evil only through Christ.

It is discouraging to see decent human beings strike out against these evils, like a sleeper annoyed by a fly buzzing near. Because they are asleep, they do not see the fly, they miss it, and the fly returns again and again. In the same manner, the evils which engulf us seem to rise and fall, to sink back and rise again. Crime and Communism, fraud and treachery, these evils are always around us. Mankind cannot prevail against them because we are asleep. Then, how do we awaken? We awaken by becoming aware of Christ, by arising in His Presence. While he is asleep, man cannot know Christ, who appears only as a distant and an unrealised fantasy. But when man awakes, he sees that Christ is not some sort of phantom, but a living, vibrant Presence which transforms everything into a splendid instrument of the Deity.

Without Christ's radiance, man is only a figment of himself, and it is this figment which is overcome by evil, which becomes the prey of crime, Communism, and disease. And yet this figment can call itself Christian without knowing Christ. God is not mocked. Do not mock God by calling yourself a Christian if you are not fighting Christ's battle against Satan. You must become a True Knight of Christ, if you are to be a Christian. It cannot be accomplished by singing a few hymns, listening to a minister tell you that Christ was a Communist, or donating money to churches to finance drug orgies and street battles against the police.

THE TRUE KNIGHT OF CHRIST

The True Knight of Christ distinguishes himself, because his every action is in praise of Christ. His life belongs to Christ, and then, and only then, does he become a true individual, because one cannot become a true individual, who is true to himself, unless he is first true to Christ. This is what is meant by the saying, "The Kingdom of God is within you."

The first thing that the True Knight of Christ learns is that it is Christ, and Christ alone, who can lead man into the world, make him aware of the world, and allow him to become a living part of the world. But isn't this materialism, isn't this Marxism, this becoming part of the world? No because in materialism, or scientific materialism, as Marx calls it, one does not become part of the world, one merely becomes a slave of the world. This is why Communism is slavery, while Christ means freedom.

The life of Christ contains everything that man needs to know, everything that he must know if he is to transcend himself. To become a spiritual force, one must first become material. Christ teaches us, first, how to become a positive part of the material world, and second, how to transcend it. And one cannot transcend the world without learning what the world is. That is why Christ was known, first of all, as a teacher. And the first thing that one learns about the world is that nothing has changed since the crucifixion of Christ. The Sanhedrin which met to order His physical execution is still firmly in charge of the lives of the masses, the gentiles are still blindly and stupidly in the grasp of evil. But this does not mean that Christ has failed L. It means that we have failed, and are failing Christ, that His sacrifice has not yet come to fruition among us, and we deny Christ in everything that we do.

CRIPPLED GENTILES

Why are gentiles cripples? Because they deny Christ in meekly accepting the evil reign of the Elders of Zion, the Devil's High Commission in charge of evil on earth, because they refuse to open their eyes to the world around them. In order to understand the great principles of evil which guide everything in the modern world, we must realize that only cripples are satisfactory to these principles of evil, the whole man, the healthy man is an abomination to the principles of evil. Thus, we are born whole and healthy, we are an abomination to evil, and every influence in our lives brings to hear the principles of evil, we are educated in every way to become cripples, to deny Christ.

Many people have been shocked by the discovery that in India, healthy children are inducted f into the profession of begging by being mutilated by their elders, having horrible sores scraped into their bodies and infected, or by having an arm or a leg cut off. But why should we be horrified by this when everything in our society is devoted to the same principle, of crippling the children so that they cannot know Christ, so that they can become acceptable to the principles of evil? Children are taught to ignore God's universe, to become blinded to the radiance of Christ, and it is these mutilated gentiles who become adults, fit only for the purposes of evil, and unable to acknowledge the Presence of Jesus Christ.

ACKNOWLEDGING CHRIST

To know Christ is as easy as opening a door, and as difficult as climbing the most treacherous precipice. We often hear of people who "accept Christ", as though He were some sort of handout given at the church door for the payment of a small fee, and we hear of other people who 'believe in Christ", as though they were signing some sort of contract, or entering into a real estate agreement, whereby the party of the second part acknowledges that the party of the first part is the Son of God, etc., etc. Now, this sort of thing does not affect Christ one way or the other; as a meaning less gesture, it is simply that, and it affects no one. It certainly does "the parties of the second part" no good whatsoever. We also hear of people who have "found Christ", as though He were some sort of diamond lying in the dirt, and these people were strolling along, with their eyes on the ground, as usual, and they picked Him up. Now, these are the kind of false trails which the Devil proliferates everywhere, and which you can turn your back on once you "know" Christ. The first step is to acknowledge the possibility of knowing Him, and of allowing this knowledge to be the principal influence in your life.

THE UNATTAINABLE CHRIST

Most theology either explicitly or implicitly presents

Christ as unattainable, or unapproachable, but who can he negotiated with through chosen representatives. This too is negated by the life of Christ on earth. When was Christ ever unapproachable or unattainable? The very lesson of Christ's material presence was that He was available to the masses. Also, why would He withdraw from the masses, and allow Himself to he approached only through representatives, many of whom have exhibited the grossest human weaknesses, and who became susceptible to the temptations of drunkenness, adultery, dope, and Communism?

Christ has never shut Himself off from us, but, because we shut ourselves off from Him, we are eager to believe that He is unapproachable, because this excuses us from knowing Him. How do we deny Him? By every opportunity which is given us to become a positive force against Satan, by placing ourselves on the wrong side in the exquisite polarization of the forces of good and evil. It is too easy to be enlisted in the forces of evil without realizing it, merely because we refuse to question, we refuse to see, we refuse to awaken. Many of those whom we accept as "pillars of society", such as government and business leaders, and persons prominent in education and the church, are either knowing or unwitting transmission belts for the forces of evil.

We cannot, we must not, forget that we are surrounded by evil in every aspect of our earthly lives. The world may be a pleasant, sunny place, the "pillars of society" may seem to be working for the good of all, even if we can see that they are wrecking the lives of many people, and the ministers may seem to be delivering positive messages of uplift and goodwill. But, if things were what they seem, would Christ have had to come among us, saying, "Woe to Ye, Pharisees and hypocrites!"

Now we too must cry out, Woe to ye, Pharisees and hypocrites! One of the great factors in the reign of evil is the admonition that one must be "nice". One cannot state the truth about the princes of darkness who now hold commanding positions. But was this Christ's way? Rather, from the beginning of His mission, did He not enter into the stronghold of the Elders of Zion, and challenge them, until they overcame their amazement and ordered His execution? One cannot prevail against the rule of darkness, if one strikes half-hearted blows. One cannot be a soldier in the Army of Christ if one fears to "alienate" people. Everyone who lives without Christ is already alienated, how can people be offended whose every act is an offence? And what is more offensive than the reign of the princes of darkness, what is more horrible than the lives of those without Christ, who, without His protection, are slowly killed, murdered every day, murdered over and over again, until at last, the zombie-like shells, drained by one atrocity after another, at last fall empty to the ground and are pronounced "dead"?

One cannot be "polite" to the forces of evil, because one who lives in Christ makes no concessions, he hews to the line, because the model is not far off. Nor are "good works" the answer. Involving oneself in good works in one's community is not a challenge to the forces of evil, and all too often, such activities are engaged in to avoid Christ, to avoid going beyond oneself, while pampering the insatiable ego, and indulging one's vanity. Now, pride and vanity are not in themselves wrong, if one has something to be proud of. But no one can be proud who has denied Christ, who has closed himself in, and who has settled down to the endless treadmill which is life without Christ, a dreary round of pointless deeds which do not and cannot lead to anything beyond the self.

RESURRECTION

The belief in resurrection should be measured against one's self-knowledge, one's understanding of what one is, and of what one has done with one's life. Now, does anyone really desire to be resurrected into the role that he now plays, through time without end? And does anyone really believe that the processes of life and death, no matter how imperfectly or how variously they are presented in the half-thought philosophical meanderings available to us, have ever been described as continuing in absolute stagnation, closed to change?

The desire to be reinstated at one's present level is based upon fear of the unknown, the sensible supposition that, rather than take a chance on something worse, one should make a play for holding onto what one now has at hand through luck, inheritance, work or other happenstance. This fear of the unknown is universal among those who have ignored Christ, but for those who have become aware of Christ, this fear vanishes. There is no longer the pathetic hope that one will retain one's frantic hold upon a particular, wretched fragment of existence, this now, this insignificant moment of time and space. Most people, if they would face the present honestly, would admit that a resurrection on their own terms would be an admission of failure. Fortunately, God does not ask us about this, He does not penalize us where we, through our own choice, would penalize ourselves.

HUMILITY

One of the aspects of knowing Christ is the attainment of true humility. By humility, we do not mean the abandoning of false pride, or of self-abnegation before others, because true humility in Christ, takes no account of the opinions of others. Being humble does not mean that one willingly accepts a lesser position in life, or that one acknowledges the pride and the self- importance of others.

The humility which is attained through knowing Christ means, first of all, that one begins to understand one's self. One also begins to understand others. This self-understanding soon generates respect from others, although this is not a conscious goal of humility. By understanding one's place in the universe, one is no longer deluded by false goals or material values, and one is prepared to take up the work. The first thing that we realize through humility in Christ is that heretofore, one's role has been very meager, that one has given very little of oneself.

This realization allows one to accept facts which are unacceptable to most men. For instance, few men are likely to acknowledge that they have been getting a free ride through life, that everything they know or use has been the contribution of others, achievements which have been arrived at through hard work and sacrifices of their predecessors. Thus, the Confucian saying, "What whiteness will you add to this whiteness?" What will you contribute?

When one has attained humility through Christ, it becomes easy to admit that one has brought nothing to life, and this prepares one to make a genuine contribution. Now, the material world often tries to convince men that what they are doing is worthwhile. And it is worthwhile, for what it is, a limited endeavour confined to the material world. A prosperous businessman once tried, somewhat desperately, to convince me that he was improving other people's lives by selling them modern appliances. I replied that there was no reason for him to justify himself to me, and that I did not doubt his sincerity.

However, I told him, you may realize that everything that one does is only a prelude to knowing Christ. I know about all that, he said, preparing for life after death. Not at all, I said. You must prepare to live here on earth. Life in Christ is life in life, You don't have to die to win, you only have to live.

I think I understand, he said. You mean that what I'm doing is not really living. It's living, I said, but it isn't the life you were meant to know. You wouldn't accept inferior merchandise from a manufacturer, don't accept an inferior life for yourself, a life without Christ. This doesn't mean that you should renounce material existence, Christ is not against materialism, He doesn't advocate that we go back to living in caves and wearing animal skins. Going forward, that's Christ, progress is Christ, but materialism as an end in itself is not progress, it's retrogression, and that's why the Communist system, which proclaims materialism, can't make a go of it. It's a very common misconception that living in Christ means giving up everything. But you don't give up anything, you add to what you have, you give meaning to the material part of your life because it is no longer an end in itself. You open yourself up and let the splendour of God's universe envelope you in all of its glory.

ANIMATION

The principal factor of our earthly existence is that we are animated, that is, we are given spirit. Many people have become so dejected by the evil which surrounds them that their animation is gone, they no longer seem to have "life". But the human machine not only is animated from without by divine forces, it is also capable of animating itself from within. And when the princes of darkness have almost succeeded in vanquishing the divine forces within us, that is when the self can rise up and proclaim itself, can renew its own animation. Everything in the material world is designed to exploit us, to drain us and to defeat us, and to maintain oneself against these forces is to win a splendid victory. It is this which explains the quite meteoric rise of some persons from very undistinguished origins, such as Joan of Arc, those who have given their animation full play, and it also explains the lack of achievement in many of those from whom we expect great things because they have been born to wealth or position, but who do nothing with their lives, simply because they lack animation.

DIVINE PROTECTION

An omnipresent force in human life is divine protection. In the formative years of this era, a more open time, this divine protection was manifested plainly to mankind, as the ascended masters appeared to men in moments of great peril, and exerted their influence (which was not always decisive), on behalf of their charges. Early Sanskrit writings describe the masters hovering over battlefields in their machines, observing and sometimes influencing events.

As man progressed, such appearances became inadvisable, for many reasons, not the least of which was the necessity for man's self-reliance, rather than looking to the heavens for divine assistance. Therefore, the masters remained invisible, and made their influence felt at crucial times, without manifesting themselves. Faith in divine assistance could be but half of the equation, with faith in man's own abilities as the solution, or the other half. All too often, man has either professed a complete reliance upon God, with no corresponding responsibility here, or he denied God and personalized all faith in himself, a materialistic concept which is known in modern times as communism.

Now, the one, immaterial religious fanaticism, gives as poor results as its opposite number, the materialist fanaticism of the Communist. in both cases, the essential ingredient, man's faith in himself, becomes misdirected, and is no longer a constructive force. Thus, any system of government which centralizes itself either in a theological, or an immaterial basis, or in a materialist and anti-theological basis, is equally maleficent in its effect upon the people. We must remember that no governmental system has ever been devised which could afford to encourage man's self-reliance, because this native ability, which would develop in an amazing geometrical ratio, would soon make any government obsolete. For one thing, it would bring us to the idealistic but never-invoked goal of the Communists, the withering away of the State.

Now, it is quite trite that any system of government which released the power of the people would soon be obsolete, but it has never happened, because every system of government devised by man has fallen prey to the forces of evil, it has become an instrument of the Devil. We live under a governmental system which in every aspect is the embodiment of true evil, and if we dared to speak honestly about it, we would have to admit that it is insane. In living under the domination of the Devil, why is it, then, that we have not been destroyed?

The only thing which saves us from complete annihilation by the governmental forces of evil is the aura of divine protection which is still maintained over the earth. Now, those who refuse to admit the presence of this divine protection, will each and every one have had some narrow escape from death. But we do not rely on such happenstances. This writer has survived eight attempts to murder him, attempts which were launched, not by bungling amateurs, but by highly professional members of criminal syndicates. But this is not what is referred to. We refer to the whole fabric of modern existence, in which man, with his highly developed sources of energy, is surrounded everywhere, at home, at work, and in the open fields, by tremendous death-dealing forces of electricity, explosives and machines which can crush him to a pulp. We continue to exist as on the edge of a volcano, which does not erupt. The electric wiring which fills our homes does not short circuit and burn us up; the tanks of fuel do not explode; the millions of automobiles rushing past each other, hubcap to hubcap, do not collide with death-dealing force.

Accidents occur, yes, but only a tiny part of the percentage which we might expect from the nature of these forces and energies. We are sitting on vast stores of nuclear weapons which could destroy the earth, but they do not, although there are many agents of the Devil in modern governments who would not hesitate to destroy the world with these weapons. They do not do so because they are restrained by divine protection, because God holds them back. The Devil is not yet strong enough to wreak his will upon us. In considering the tremendous dangers which surround man during every hour of his existence, only a fool would deny the presence of divine protection.

DRUGS

Why has the use of drugs been so widespread in the history of man? Man needs these drugs, and he takes them because he is forced to, not because they are a pleasant end in themselves, or because he has a natural affinity for them. The drugs offer relief—but relief from what? Is life really so terrible? Yes, life without Christ, the state in which most men live, is a terrible thing. It is a state so exasperating that man is driven to seek any means of relief. This writer has known alcoholics, drug addicts, and other slaves of habits, in various strata, among the very rich and among the very poor. None of them could be said to obtain any lasting pleasure from their addictions, but they needed even a temporary relief.

Life is terrible, and drugs do offer some relief, but it is only temporary, and this forces the user into addiction. Christ also offers relief from the terrible, the Satanic aspects of human existence, but this relief is not temporary and leads to no addiction. Is Christ merely another drug, then? No, Christ is not a drug, nor is the Christian religion an opiate of the people, except when its practitioners use it so.

It was the easily observed result that people experienced such tremendous relief through Christ which led Marx to the mistaken belief that religion was the opium of the people, because this relief was obviously more potent than the strongest known narcotic. However, Marx could not understand this, because, as a Jew, he had been brought up in hatred of Jesus Christ, he could not fathom the relief that Christ could bring. Also, Marx saw Christ only in an older, a more primitive society, the early years of the Industrial Age. Does this mean that Christ offers less relief in our modern technological age? On the contrary, Christ is needed more and more in our industrialized society, because the tremendous pressures which man is forced to endure in this society are conforming him to the machine and moulding him to a machine-like existence. As a result, man suffers more today than he did in the agricultural society. Then, he had to work out of doors in bitter weather, but the suffering was less intense. The industrial society, on the other hand, inflicts considerable mental suffering, in the process of converting men into useful machines, so that the worker needs aspirin, alcohol, narcotics, and any other available relief to survive in this hellish atmosphere.

And does Christ bring relief even from the torments of the industrial society? Yes, Christ is the Way, and the way He offers is as viable in the industrial society as it was in the more primitive agricultural world. There have been dark hours in the history of man, but never so dark as today. Never has man been so nakedly presented with the most brutal facts of existence. It is for this reason that man now seeks, at any costs, to maintain his condition of sleep, that he must use any means, drugs, work, sex, anything, to keep his eyes shut against the hell which surrounds him. Nov, in the moment of knowing Christ, there is a terrible awakening, a moment so fraught with horror that few men are willing to face it. Yet one cannot know Christ without looking at our world, without acknowledging that we are living in Hell, in the power of the Devil, because one must endure this terrible vision before knowing Him. It is a terrible decision to ask of anyone, knowing what it demands. This writer has known men who, upon realizing the awful conditions under which they had lived, collapsed with nervous breakdowns, and entered a state of shock from which they never emerged. Now, these were mature men, responsible men who had carried out successful business enterprises. They were men who thought that they knew life, that they had seen everything, and were fully aware of the world in which they lived, men who could not be surprised by anything. Yet they had really managed to keep their eyes closed, to function without acknowledging the Hell in which they lived. Nor were they asked to know Christ, they were merely advised, as one intelligent person advises another, of some of the facts of our existence, of the circumstances of our lives, that we are surrounded by noise, by fire, by evil, in a living Hell. The revelation was too much for them, and they went into shock.

It is for this reason that many men who know the facts of our existence, and know the shock it would bring to others, therefore remain silent, because it is too dangerous to expose others to this knowledge, especially if they are not prepared to know Christ, the only antidote to the Hell in which we live. And there are others, many, many others, who, fully aware of the Hell in which we live, resolve to become part of this world, who admit that they are doomed, and they cooperate in maintaining this Hell, and participate in the conspiracies of the Devil. Principal among these are the Jews, those who demanded the Crucifixion of Jesus, but since they are a small number in the world of men, they cannot carry out the work of the

Devil without the active assistance of millions of deluded and hypnotized gentiles, who have denied Christ, and who now exist as the tools of the Devil in maintaining Satan's Hell on earth.

DENYING CHRIST

Many of these gentiles feel guilty for denying Christ, and are fearful of being punished by Him. And they are punished, but not by Christ, for it is not Christ's Will to add to the suffering of mankind, hut to relieve it In denying Christ, these gentiles are punished, but their punishment consists solely in not knowing Christ, in living without His aid. These deluded persons expect punishment, and they receive it, but at their own bands, and not by the Will of Christ.

Other people believe that Christ punishes men, and they point to the example of the Jews, who have suffered torments on earth ever since they demanded the Crucifixion of Christ. But here again, Christ has not ordered the punishment of the Jews. Everything that they have endured has been because of their own nature, and because of their own acts, which inflamed others against them, and brought about their punishment. just as their nature demanded the Crucifixion of Christ, so their native has caused them to commit harm against peoples among which they have lived, and incited these peoples to rise against them. Here again, do not mock God by attributing the evil motives of hate and revenge to the Pure Nature of Christ.

The concept of punishment itself is merely an unhealthy manifestation of egotism. The warden of Sing Sing prison remarked, after many years in that post, "I have never met a criminal who did not wish to be punished." It is this egotism which leads men to suppose that God is concerned with the slightest misstep which we make. How could this be? God is concerned, yes, but He is not a policeman whose only profession is crime arid punishment. We can expect God's attention only when we -have done something worthy of His attention, when we have contributed something to His world.

It is because God cannot become actively involved in the slightest misstep of each of us that Christ was sent to help us. But here again, we have been prevented from knowing Christ by our own egotism. We wanted Christ to approve what we were, but Christ was concerned with what we could become. When we demand approval of what we are, we ignore a fundamental law of God's universe, that everything changes. It can change for the better, or it can change for the worse, and in knowing Christ, we can make the correct decision. Instead, we have demanded that He become involved in the hopelessness of our present state, and it is this concern which has bogged down Christianity for two thousand years, the concern with sin, the obsession of our egotism that we must be punished for what we have done, as though what we have clone is that

Important.

Christ tried to awaken man from sleep, to reveal to man what he could become, and release ourselves from the miserable things that we are. Yet, two thousand years later, we are still mired down in the same hopeless egotism, still blind to the meaning of Christ.

THE HARMONY OF THE SPHERES

We have often heard the phrase, "the harmony of the spheres", as though it were some sort of childish fantasy which could have no relation to our lives. At the same time, we are asked to live "harmoniously", without friction, in a legal world, and in accordance with established laws. What we do not realize is that our established laws originated in the harmony of the universe, although many of these laws have become twisted through the influence of the Devil, until our legal system is the principal instrument of the Devil on earth, and lawyers and judges are his most important agents, so that men are prosecuted for being hard-working, decent citizens, and rewarded for being thieves, rapists and murderers. For many years, the Supreme Court of the United States has acted with vicious haste to punish decent Americans, while setting free the most hardened criminals to steal and kill as they desire. Now, is this not the work of the Devil?

Here again, we must remind ourselves of the First Precept, to go beyond, to look underneath and see what underlies the apparent and the everyday world. There is a harmony in the United States Constitution, which was written by men who were aware of the harmony of the spheres, and for that reason, the Constitution has been under attack for almost two hundred years, and the agents of the Devil have done everything within their power to amend it, pervert it, and make it an instrument of evil.

All of the disharmony which exists in the United States today is due to government officials who are in the power of the Devil, and who prevent us from living by the divine harmony of the United States Constitution. Those who work against the Constitution do the work of the Devil, but if we can live by our Constitution and its divine harmony, we can bring order into our lives, so that we can go further. The Constitution is only a step in the right direction, a step which makes possible other steps, to enter into the greater harmony.

We have seen examples of this in the men who have been called "geniuses". Now, a genius is simply one who creates, and who has released his creative energy by coming into contact with the divine harmony. We like to believe that only a tiny fraction of mankind can ever become a genius, that a Shakespeare or a Goethe only appears among many hundreds of millions of human beings.

This, like so much else that we believe, is false. The possibility of doing wholesome, creative work, of becoming a genius, is open to anyone who accepts divine harmony and who comes to know Christ. If this sounds like a simple task, it is not. First, one must rule out every falsehood in one's life, in order to accept divine harmony. Since we maintain our lives by a multitude of falsehoods, this means abandoning the shibboleths by which we delude ourselves and maintain our condition of sleep. Because Christ is Truth, this can be done, and it must be done. Nor is it beyond our capabilities, because, in our inmost being, we know every falsehood for what it is, an expression of disharmony. We accept these falsehoods because we think we may injure ourselves or others by renouncing them.

These falsehoods must be expelled from our lives just as a medicine expels germs, and then we become a finer instrument, we begin to know the harmony of the spheres. But how, one asks, do we recognize this harmony? No one lives without some consciousness of the divine harmony. Even the most brutish of us is occasionally overcome by a great sensibility, in which poignant moments of truth and beauty are experienced, in which every care vanishes, and one is borne by a splendid sensation. In fact, this is just what the user of drugs is seeking, because he does not know how to reach the divine harmony.

A drug is a mechanical attempt to know ecstasy, a

chemical influence upon the organism which is expected to achieve a divine result. Because this attempt fails, the user of drugs tries again and again, and becomes an addict, Drug addiction can be overcome by achieving divine harmony through knowing Christ.

Prayer is another attempt to reach divine harmony, but it is usually mechanical in its aspiration, or attempted because of some mechanical desire, and it becomes nothing more than a method of concentration, which may or may not be useful in attaining the mechanical desire. If it is not approached through meditation, it is rarely of any genuine use.

YOUTH

One of the most talked-about problems today is the problem of south. We hear much of the predilection of young people for ignoring the rat race, and leading what is called "an irresponsible life". These are the people who are known today as "hippies". Now, what does "irresponsibility" mean? It means, failing to respond. If young people are not answering, is it not because they have not been asked the question?

The question is, "How are they to live?" And the answer which the older generations supply for them,—"They must live just as we do." Now, the parents would not ask their children to live as men did in the Stone Age, or in the

Babylonian Empire, or like the Lapps in Finland, because they would not expect their children to accept such a mode of existence, But, in asking their children to live as they do, the parents are asking the young people to accept an already obsolete mode of existence. The moving finger writes, and having writ, moves on. But if the mode of existence changes with each generation, what standards does anyone have, what permanent values can we hold onto? The permanent value is Christ, and in not knowing Christ, everyone is caught between the changing modes of existence, fearful and experiencing a sense of loss, like an Eskimo hunter on an ice floe which is rapidly drifting away from the shore.

Now, what age do we live in We have long been told that we are approaching the close of the Piscean Age, the Era of the Fish, when Christ came to us as a Fisher of Men, recruiting His apostles among the fisher folk, and teaching them to become fishers of men. But this period of our existence is ending, and we are approaching the Aquarian Age, a different time, in which people will live differently. Quite without anyone telling them to, the young people are already adopting an Aquarian mode of existence.

What sort of life is the Aquarian mode? It is a more communal existence, in which the amassing of private property is no longer the sole reason for existence, in which sexual customs are more open, and in which people refuse to consider each other solely on the grounds of their armor, or their shielding of the self. The reason for shaggy hair, unkept appearance, and slovenly clothing among these young people is that they are prophets, and harbingers of the approaching Aquarian Age. Now, people will not live this way in the coming age, anymore than conventional Christians of the Piscean Age go about in rags, with hair falling to their feet. Young people today are exaggerating, because they are trying to tell us what they themselves do not know, that we are in the Aquarian Age.

For this reason, the young people are against the Vietnam War. Now, the Vietnam war is a war like any other, then why this furious protest? The young people protest because the Vietnam war is an anomaly, it is a hangover from the Piscean Age, things will no longer be done this way. Those who have money and power in this close of the Piscean Age are not trying to hold people back, they are simply continuing to do things the same way, because it is the only way they know. And while they are standing on the deck of the sinking ship, they are talking confidently of another long and profitable voyage, while the waters of the ocean already swirl at their feet. We have not realized that the doctrine of Communism, or a more communal society, was a harbinger of the approach of the Aquarian Age. However, once it was seized upon by Karl Marx, and became influenced by the warped mind of the Jew, it became another instrument of the Devil, no one could any longer understand what it had meant. World War II was the end of the Piscean Age, and since then, young people have been very disturbed, because they have been asked to lead us into the Aquarian Age without any guidelines, on pure instinct. Twenty years ago, this writer was already leading an Aquarian existence in New York, in which people were allowed to come in, to share what food and lodging there was, without any demands made or expectation of payment, and many others were living this way, in what was termed a "beatnik" mode, and much later, the "hippie" mode.

This mode of existence is open to many abuses, particularly when people do not are the new mode. In the same way, young people are marching about, shouting slogans, and waving banners without much idea of what they are doing. Now they are retreating from this into a more Aquarian mode, beginning to live for themselves. The young people lost nothing by giving up this struggle, because they could not gain anything by it, while the Communists, who had obtained some benefit from the agitation, tried vainly to keep it going.

Can the Aquarian Age be like this, asks the horrified citizen, as he looks at the unwashed youths, living in filthy places, and subsisting upon drugs? Of course not. This is a transitional stage, and these young people are refugees in time, displaced persons caught between the Piscean and the Aquarian Age. They use drugs to ease the pain of transition. Instinctively, they recognize that the Piscean Age has been a time of horrors, in which Christ was more and more estranged from man. The Piscean Age is ending in unrelieved horror, in filth, in noise, and in total bondage to the Prince of Darkness. Having known a Master in the Piscean Age, I have no regrets in seeing the end of it, as those who come after will not be so much in themselves, but will be much more in each other.

The Piscean Age degenerated into an age of aggression, and for this reason, elaborate protective devices were set up. In time, these protective devices, these castles, these weapons and armour, dwarfed the humanitarian concepts with which Christ had begun this Age. The Piscean man became frozen in hideous trappings of power, power which was sought for self-protection, but which became the goal of all existence.

With the coming of the Aquarian Age; the young people reject the armor and the castles of the Piscean Age, they reject personal power, because it is not needed when aggression is abandoned. But without power, how can we defend ourselves? We defend ourselves through Christ, because in Him we can trust each other. And in rejecting the trappings of the Piscean Age, the young people the hippies, are going to extremes, because they do not know why they are rejecting these things. And in rejecting the antiseptic middle-class homes which produced them in a sterile atmosphere, the young people for the moment embrace personal uncleanliness, but once they realize where they are, and what they are, they will not need these rejections, these drugs, these crutches with which they seek to ease the transitional period. In any case, we cannot overlook the fact that the young people today who are accepting the new age, and are living in its precepts, are the new saints, for an incredible beauty shines out from those who are truly in the Aquarian Age, a beauty to which we remain blind only if we are irrevocably committed to the travesties of the Piscean Age.

BECOMING AN ADULT

One of the problems which faces every young person is becoming an adult. How does one become an adult? This is simple, or so the world tells us. One becomes an adult by assuming responsibilities, by marrying and by raising a family. How simple, and how limited! Throughout eternity, man will beget man, as the sole fulfilment of human responsibility. Now, does anyone really believe this? Is this all that is expected of us? No, much more is expected of us, but we do not respond. We do not respond because we do not know Christ, and if we do not know Christ, we cannot make any progress whatsoever.

Why is this? Because the world is filled with false trails, with misleading dogma, and misinformation. We cannot find the way, we do not know what to believe, until we know Christ, and once we know Christ, we know the Truth, for the Truth is Christ. And once we know the way, we can progress, our sentences are repealed, the sentence of remaining where one is.

And once we know Christ, once we are able to progress, what is this progress? It means that for the first time, we become awake, a sentient being, one who is aware. Nov, once you are awake, once you know Christ, you find yourself in a strange situation. You are awake in a world in which everyone else is asleep. What shall you do? Awaken the others? Or remain quiet, without disturbing them?

The choice is not yours to make. First, you cannot awaken the others. They can be awakened only by knowing Christ. You cannot assume the duties of Christ, you can not take on the burdens of others. They can awaken only by following their own road, as you have followed your own road.

What does knowing Christ mean, in material rewards? You will see, in your awareness, that sleepwalkers and human robots are rewarded for their quiescence, they share richly in the rewards of this world, They are given great power, and some of them great riches. And yet you, who know Christ, do not receive these things. Why is this? Because their progress is not progress, and their riches are as nothing, because this wealth is only of this world, and must be spent in this world.

These mechanical men get to the top, but what is their situation? To understand the material world, think of a cesspool, a stagnant body in which the lighter pieces of offal, as they decay on the bottom, begin to rise, ascending through the muck until they break through to the surface, and ride easily upon the green slime. Now, this offal is on the top, it has arrived, and it will be satisfied and content with its good fortune.

This is the situation of those who have become successful in the material world. But you, who see the material world for what it is, see nothing more than a piece of offal which has risen through the muck, becoming lighter as it becomes more decayed and rotten. And this offal begins to realize at some point, and vaguely, that it has not gotten anywhere, and that the wealth and power of its position seems pointless. The government officials, leaders in educational and religious groups, and millionaires find that they have no real power, and they end up by despising themselves and the other who have also risen to the crest of the slime. And of course they are not going anywhere. Progress, for those who know Christ, means taking part in the earth's mission, which is to assume a greater role in God's Universe, and its rightful place in All Worlds. But this cannot be done until many are awake, and know Christ.

OUR MISSION

What is the mission of earth? For those who are asleep, this question has no significance, but as mankind begins to awaken, an event which may occur with great speed, it becomes relevant. Hermann °berth has written, "This is the goal: To make available for life every place where life is possible. To make inhabitable all worlds as yet uninhabitable, and all life purposeful. One thing we do not know; is sentient life (awareness) beginning for the first time in the universe, or is it ending here? This is one of the things which we may discover, once we devote ourselves to the goal, to make sentient life a universal thing."

Whatever we may be able to accomplish will be useless unless it is done through one's knowledge of Christ, because we will be making the first step towards liberating the universe from a longstanding slavery and an evil dream, because we have not yet come to understand what part of the dream we are living. The knowledge of the world which we arrive at through observation or experience is of no use without a sense of form. It was this to which Coomaraswamy referred when he said, "The source of truth is not empirical perception (pratyaksha), but an inwardly known model which at the same time gives form to knowledge and is the cause of knowledge,"

LOVE

Love is not only the highest emotion of which man is capable; it is also the most basic one. Everything which is positive in the polarity of existence is based upon love. However, our understanding of live is based primarily upon misconceptions of one sort or another. First of all, we consider love primarily as a familial relationship, the love of man and wife, and of parents and children. But this is a beginning, it is the first step. Most people consider it the end of love, and exclude love which is not based upon the familial relationship, or a prelude to it. And because they consider it the end of love, and not the beginning, they do not realize that the love of the man and the woman is a step towards that love which is in Christ, and everything which is built in this world is built upon that love which is in Christ.

Now, this is not new; we have heard this many times, but do we perceive it? What does it mean? It means that, in love, as in all things, we do not stand still; we either progress, or we fall back. Now, those who have built a family relationship, do they go on to Christ's love, or do they fall back? They fall hack, because they do not know how to go ahead in Christ's love. They have become part of society, because they have achieved the family relationship, and because they have been approved by society, but society is not Christ, being part of society is not being part of Christ, knowing one's role in society does not mean that one knows one's role in Christ.

In all this, know that Christ is the way, Christ is the open door. Christ does not close the door, Christ does not say, remain where you are. A static, ignorant society is not Christ, a society which moves ahead in its knowledge of Christ, this is Christ.

ATMOSPHERE

To know Christ means that one becomes a true individual, one becomes true to oneself, one knows oneself, by knowing Christ. And, by becoming an individual, one becomes part of Cod's world, because those who do not know Christ are not part of God's world. They are in the world, but they are not of the world, hence the saying, 'out of this world", those who are not part of God's world, and who are not part of His Atmosphere.

What is the condition of the world today? It is a world in which pollution of every kind threatens the continued existence of humanity, in which almost every act of man further pollutes the atmosphere, and in which the Jewish Hell bomb threatens to so pollute the earth that all human life will become impossible.

Now, everything that we do affects the atmosphere because we are part of the atmosphere. Our breath and our exudations are part of the atmosphere, and the atmosphere is part of us. By polluting the atmosphere, we pollute ourselves, and why do we pollute ourselves? We pollute ourselves because we do not know Christ. Christ is the way, because Christ shows us bow to live with ourselves without destroying ourselves. When we become destructive and pollute our atmosphere, we are working for the Devil, we have become part of Satan's Empire, but when we can live in God's world without polluting the atmosphere, we are moving ahead in our knowledge of Christ.

WHY CHRIST?

In the history of mankind, our problems have always seemed insurmountable, and beyond man's powers to solve alone. As a result, we have looked for supernatural aid from non-material sources. There have been prophets and prophecies, spiritual leaders who have attracted vast followings, and promises of varying degrees of absolution and redemption. In this melange, why Christ?

First of all, Christ is the only one whom we know to have transcended earthly existence. Second, Christ is the only one who has maintained a Presence, whom we can know. Other spiritual leaders are represented by idols, by temples, by caves, by relics, but Christ has no need of them.

Third, Christ maintained a spiritual level of work, never becoming mired in the repressive aspects of material life. The "modern" movement in Christianity has sought to do precisely that, to bring Christ down from His spiritual level and to mire Him in materialist existence.

Look at the Miracle of the Loaves and the Fishes. We think of this as a worthwhile charitable work, of providing the masses who had a right to be fed, but Christ did not intend this miracle as just another meal, one more distending of stomachs with necessary food. He enacted this miracle to impress upon us the miraculous nature of life, but instead, of grasping His lesson that all life is a miracle, we gobble down the material sustenance as a purely material phenomenon and ignore His Message.

And once we have "chosen" Christ, after we have examined His credentials and decided that His credit cards are up-to-date, what then? We "give" ourselves to Christ, with the immodest conception that we are offering Him a pearl of great price, when in fact we are presenting Him with a quite worthless gift.

We cannot know Christ unless we admit that we are living in Hell, that we are worthless human beings in our present state, and that we wish to advance to Christ's conception of mankind, and that we no longer are willing to remain imprisoned in Satan's fantastic idea of man which is our life today.

In knowing Christ, of what advantage are the churches? First of all, the churches do not include knowing Christ in their mission. The most accepted church today is a polite club, whose members know and approve of one another, with that approval always subject to withdrawal, and who cooperate in a social" or a material mission. Growing in influence, however, are the churches which have found the social mission inadequate for their ambitions, and who have adopted a "social action" mission. The social action churches are in headlong flight from Christ, because they preach hate, instead of love. They accept the erroneous doctrine of Christ as a wild-eyed Communist revolutionary, whose only mission was to overthrow the established order.

Now, insofar as Christ wishes to overthrow Satan's Empire on earth, He does wish to overthrow the established order, but He does not wish to do this by setting class against class, race against race, because these are Satan's tactics of dividing and conquering. The bright-eyed priests and ministers who are inciting the Negroes to march against the white citizens and burn them out, these "Christian leaders" are doing the work of Satan on earth.

Christ will overthrow the established order by advancing man, by leaving the old order behind as a useless skin which man has outgrown, and He will advance man through people who know Christ and who therefore know themselves, who can be themselves.

All those who conform to other people's ideas of themselves, who present themselves and think of themselves only in the "image" which others have of them, these people are the tools of Satan because they cannot know Christ. And many of these people have come to this pass because they "believe" in Christ.

Now, believing in Christ is a step, but it is not the Way, it is not the Journey. It is the beginning of knowing Christ, not the end. Now, when you say that you "believe" in Christ, does it change you in any way? Of course not. Obviously there is more to be done. Believing in Christ, in the sense that you believe that one brand of corn flakes is better than another brand, this is merely exercising a choice, it does not bring you to Christ's conception of yourself, it does not release you from your bondage to Satan.

THE BIRTH OF CHRIST

On Christmas Eve, the world falls silent, the air is filled with an approaching Glory. by is this? The physical birth of Christ is a moment which the world relives each year, because the world needs this annual reminder of the Presence of Christ. Why is the Coming of Christ such an important moment in the history of man?

In order to understand this, we must realize that before the birth of Christ, human life had no meaning. Man was merely another animal, eking oat a precarious animal existence, interested only in animal survival. And so it remains with much of mankind today. But this brutish existence has been touched with Glory, It was the Coming of Christ, a Light which has illuminated all that is good and gracious in man.

Even so, much of mankind was deaf to Christ's Message.

Principal among these were the most primitive and brutish of all men, Stone Age Jews, who had persisted in a Satanic way of life in their remote desert and mountain fastnesses, living as bandits and murderers whose blood rites removed them from the pale of human civilization. Then why did Christ walk in Jewry, until the Jews sought to kill Him? Because the Jews represented the greatest challenge to Christ. If Christ could arouse the primitive Jews from their brutish existence, what a lesson this would be to the rest of mankind! Then all would be inspired to know Christ, But Satan was with his own, and the Jews preferred Satan to Christ; this was the meaning of Christ's walk in Jewry.

Christ was not rejected by the Jews, because He never reached them with His Message. They were too firmly bound lip in Satan's image to be affected by Christ's Love. And because the Jews were not affected by Christ's Love, many gentiles seized upon this as an excuse to reject Him, and to remain enmeshed in their stupid and brutish existence. And because of this rejection, Christ would not come again in that form. Instead of reaching all men, He would reach one man and one would be all. And since the days when Christ walked in Jewry, He has appeared again, the Second Coming, but the Presence of Christ has come to man the one, the individual, and not to the group. This, to know Christ is to experience the Second Corning, to have revealed unto you the Presence of Jesus Christ and the meaning of life, And the meaning of life is simply this — the animal existence which we lead as the sheep of Satan is not life, but death. In Satan's hands, we do not know life, we do not know Christ, we do not know the world. And now we must know life, we must know Christ, we must know the world, because Satan's Empire, the Hell in which we live, is drawing to its close, it has been doomed by its own iniquity. It is soon to perish, because it was never meant to be a world, it has never been a world, and it has no reason for continued existence. It has never been more than a figment of Satan's imagination, and this figment contains a touch point, that when the burden of evil reaches a certain point in Satan's Empire, it will destroy itself. This is the explanation of the Jewish Hell bomb, which is already fused to destroy the world, it is an essential part of Satan's imaginary world of evil.

And when Satan's Empire disappears in a burst of flame, what will remain? Then those who have not known Christ, those who have never lived, they will disappear with Satan's Empire. But those who have known Christ, those who have known life, those who have known the world, they will live, because life begins where Satan's Empire ends.

THE SUFFERING OF CHRIST

Throughout the world, Christians celebrate Christ on the Cross, the Crucified Christ, the Defeated Christ, the Suffering Christ. Now, know this — Christ did not suffer. Because man lives in Hell, and knows only suffering, he supposes that Christ suffered great agonies on the Cross. But Christ's only agony on the Cross, the Passion of Jesus Christ, was that He had not reached man, that the Stone Age Jews had prevailed for Satan. There was no physical suffering. A Pure Nature cannot know physical pain — the Pure Nature of Christ could not know suffering on the Cross.

Man, seeing Christ on the Cross, supposed that He was suffering great pain, and thinking this, he had the opportunity to rush forward and relieve Christ's suffering by offering himself to Christ. But man did not do this, and Christ rose up to Heaven, leaving man behind to suffer, to the suffering to which man had condemned himself because he did not know Christ. To this day, the Jews have seen to it that the most widely encountered representation of Christ is that of Christ nailed to the Cross, and, presumably, enduring great suffering. Now why have the Jews insisted upon this representation of Christ? To put fear of the Jews into all men, as the Persians had fear of the Jews after Esther had persuaded King Ahasuerus to slaughter his gentile subjects for the benefit of the Jews, the great Purim Festival. And b fearing the Jews, men would accept the Empire of Satan, and would not know redemption through Christ.

The image of Christ on the Cross persuades men that those who oppose the Jews will die in great agony after undergoing merciless tortures and seeing their families slain before their eyes, as the vengeance of the Jews was wreaked on Haman. And this image of Christ has served the Jews well, because it has convinced gentiles that they must live in slavery to the Jews and in bondage to Satan, without knowing Christ.

But to those who know Christ, the image of the Defeated Christ, the Crucified Christ, the suffering Christ, has no validity, for the first thing that one learns, in knowing Christ, is that Christ did not suffer. And, knowing that Christ did not suffer, one learns that one will never know suffering again, because one has overcome what is worse than pain itself, and that is the fear of pain. The Jews rule through the threat of inflicting pain, rather than the actual inflicting of suffering. They are able to do Satan's work because they have impressed the gentile their image of a suffering Christ. And those who accept the suffering Christ, they do not know Christ, they cannot know Christ, until they discover for themselves the Pure Nature of Christ, which is beyond suffering and the tortures of Satan's Hell upon earth.

And in accepting the image of Christ on the Cross, what do we do? We see, not with our own vision, but with the vision of others. We look out of the window, but we see only what the window sees, The Jew is Our window on the world, he seeks to present the world to 115, distorted and coloured with his peculiar vision of Satan's Empire, of Hell on earth.

THE SELF

Knowing Christ means, first of all, that there is someone there, someone to now Christ, that is, that there is a sentient being, not a mechanical man, not one who is asleep in the world. Now, knowing oneself is a precept, after all, which has been urged upon mankind by many philosophers throughout the centuries, not the least of whom was Socrates.

Knowing one's Self means that one looks at the Self. Now, what is the Self? For more of us, the Self is a handsome stranger, who rides up at dusk with a lavish equipage, and who strides in with such lordliness that we, the humble inn-keeper, dare not ask him for his credentials, or question as to who will pay the bill. And, for most of us, the Sell remains the lordly stranger, whom we are quite pleased to have staying with us, and whose enormous bills we uneasily ignore.

Now, at some point, we must make a start — we must ask the handsome stranger — Who are you? And, most important of all, we must ask him, What do you want? For this is the question to which we must know the answer, if we are ever to know the Self, and, subsequently, to know Christ.

What does the Self want? Has he come to stay with us because he has heard that this is a salubrious climate, that the service is well-maintained, the food of consistent quality? Why is he here? The answer cannot be given until the question is asked.

The Self visiting the inn-keeper, like everything which we can know, is part of the Life of Christ. The Birth of Christ in the stable, after puzzling the inn-keeper as to where he could find a place for the strangers, this is the parable of God offering a Self to the world, so that life in the world could have a meaning And the world, without wholly rejecting this Self, did not put it out altogether, as the inn-keeper found a place for Christ in the stable, so we have allowed the Self to remain, but not to become a part of us. And so we live on, without knowing the Self, without knowing Christ, and without giving a meaning to our lives.

CHAPTER TWO

SATAN'S EMPIRE

INTELLIGENT

Americans seem to be astounded at the discovery that the forces of law and order in this country are arrayed on the side of the criminals, and that such governmental organizations as the Federal Bureau of Investigation and the Central Intelligence Agency have as their principal functions the harassment of honest citizens, instead of prosecuting traitors and criminals. These organizations themselves have become groups of bandits which prey upon the workers of our nation, in the same manner as the Jews and the Mafia whom they emulate in every aspect of their operations. Why should any American be astounded at this? We know that in every rank of life, only those who have sold themselves to the Devil can hope to attain any eminence in a world which is Satan's Empire. How medieval it sounds, to sell oneself to the Devil! And how medieval it is, this world in which we live, in which Christ is ignored and millions flock to sell themselves to the Devil so that they can enjoy a few moments of comfort and prosperity.

The fact is that this is a medieval world; it is more than that, it is a prehistoric world, a world which exists Before Christ, as though He had never walked among us. The Jews denounce anything that is virtuous and true as being "medieval", because in the medieval period, they were crouched in their ghettoes, gathering their psychic forces of evil in preparation for their last onslaught against the gentiles, an onslaught which has brought them to pre-eminence today. Why is this?

In medieval times, men thought they had walled up the Devil, in confining the Jews to the ghettoes, but it was the Jews who preferred to remain in the ghettoes, until their psychic forces of evil were replenished and they could sally forth to do the work of the Devil.

Man cannot depend upon walls in combating evil. One cannot ignore the Devil as the ignoranti ignore Christ, because the Devil pushes in everywhere, he finds the least opening. Therefore, one must seek an adequate defence against the Devil, and the only defence is to know Christ. Nevertheless, men erected such defences as they could, and this is why the principle of republicanism is so important in the American heritage, and in our Christian heritage. The rights of the individual, and *res publica* — the things that are public.

The first step in eroding the life of the individual is to destroy all of his privacy, to intrude upon his serenity in Christ in every possible way, and to use every department of *re publica,* the public existence, to destroy his privacy and his serenity. Thus, the ignoranti in every level of the government use their powers to send out all sorts of agents to harass the individual, to belay him with tax agents, FBI agents, CIA agents and other disciples of evil.

Nov, we note that anyone who is leading a life of evil is ignored by these agents; he is free to carry on his evil work. Only decent and honest workers, who have some possibility of living in Christ, are the victims of these agents. Thus we see that criminals and traitors flourish unmolested in every part of our nation, while the FBI protects the criminals and the CIA subsidizes the traitors.

All violent revolutionary activities in the United States, in Latin America, and in other countries are financed with CIA funds. The CIA agents spend millions of the American taxpayers' dollars each month to finance the harangues of such revolutionaries as H. Rap Brown, men who exhort mobs to burn down the cities of America.

The FBI maintains an active alliance with the Mafia at every level of criminal activity. How could this be, one asks? You must remember that crime did not become a national problem in America until after the FBI was set up. Its first principle has been to render ineffective the law enforcement of local and state police departments, to take over their authority. Crime has become a more serious problem each year since the FBI began its operations, and in order to understand that, one must understand the personality of its ostensible leader,

CRIPPLES

The crippled ones who lead so many important fields in the United States are sometimes self-mutilated, and in other, more tragic cases, are victims of the Devil's milieu in which we live. Some of them have crippled themselves in order to be enlisted in the profitable pursuits of the great currents of evil in modern life, and they have to cripple others in order to maintain their positions, in order to satisfy the constant needs of the Devil. For this reason, we find so many professionals in education, in religion, and in government, whose only purpose in practicing their profession is to cripple others, to blind them to the splendours of God's world. Their first precept is to blind everyone to the Radiance of Jesus Christ, and often to pretend to work in His Name while denying all of His Teachings. Thus, instead of illuminating the young, these cripples blind all who come within their influence. And they reserve their praise only for other cripplers. We find the cripplers in education praising the cripplers in religion, we find the cripplers in government praising the cripplers in education, and carrying on a vast interlocking directorate of power and influence. This interlocking network of congratulating cripplers is known as "the American Establishment".

All of these people, who in themselves are the dregs of

humanity, and helpless tools of Satan, are those who head our great universities, our government programs, our museums, and other institutions which affect the daily lives of every American, yet they are so disgusting that many of those who come into personal contact with them are made physically ill. A great entertainer, who had made his own reputation without help from anyone, was asked to have lunch with the head of one of the television networks. He later said that the man, a furtive alien type, made him so ill that he twice left the table in. order to vomit.

GET RID OF THE CIA AND THE FBI

When I made a public demand, printed and circulated under my own name in 1968, that the CIA and the FBI be disbanded and their functions and files be turned over to the Counter-Intelligence Corps of the United States Army, the reaction was not the indignant one I had expected from the brainwashed American public. Instead, there was amazement that I had had the courage to denounce the two groups which have done so much to destroy the American Republic, and to subvert its laws and institutions.

RUIN OF THE CIA

Few Americans have any knowledge of the origins of these sinister groups. The Central Intelligence Agency had its beginnings in a group of Jewish Communist agitators who were expelled by the German. Government in the nineteen thirties, an act of mercy which ignored justice, since they deserved imprisonment for their treachery. These agitators were welcomed by the Jewish community in the United States, and all immigration laws were ignored to admit them without delay. The Establishment's propaganda machine immediately went into effect, hailing these criminals as "great geniuses", and "champions of democracy". Gentile professors were rudely fired and their teaching posts given to the criminals, while others were given important government posts in Washington, many in 1939, these agitators ceased their furious campaign against Germany, but when Germany fought the Soviet Union in 1941 in an effort to destroy Communism, the agitators formed an intelligence network in Washington, which became known as the Office of War Information. As usual, a nondescript gentile journalist named Elmer Davis was named to head the operation. The Jewish Communists ran it to suit themselves, Davis made good use of the unlimited credit established for him at local bars.

COMMUNIST PROPAGANDA AGENCY

Throughout World War II, the precursor of the CIA, the Office of War Information followed the official Soviet line so closely that they sometimes anticipated it, and their bosses in Moscow had to deny the stories which their henchmen were broadcasting from Washington. When the lied Army massacred many thousands of members of the Polish middle class in an atrocity at the Katyn Forest, Elmer Davis immediately went on the air to protest that the Soviets had not committed the crime. To his last day, Elmer Davis refused to admit that the Soviets had committed the horror of Katyn Forest, despite the findings of three impartial investigations which established the guilt of the Communist assassins.

Does it surprise any American that an official United States agency should become a tool of the Community Party? Let us remember that at this time, the three personal advisers of President Franklin D. Roosevelt, Harry Dexter White, Alger Hiss, and Lauchlin Currie, were all named as Communist agents. No one saw the President unless one of these three men authorized it. He was cut off from the American people by a well-organized network of Communist agents. Now the official heir of the Roosevelt mantle, Lyndon B. Johnson, is operating the same way, with the heirs of Currie, Hiss and White.

BECOMES CIA

At the end of the war, the DWI was so closely identified with the Communist Part that it was disbanded by President Truman. The Jewish Communists went back to their well-paying university posts, infecting the youth of America with their Satanic doctrines, a sowing which has reaped the harvest of demonstrations and shattered careers a generation later.

With the establishment of the State of Israel, the Jews needed an agency in Washington which would devote itself exclusively to their needs. The Jewish Communists were called back and the offal of the DWI was renamed the Central Intelligence Agency. From the outset, it was devoted largely to spying upon the Arab peoples on behalf of Israel, and these Israeli spies could not be arrested by the Arab governments, because they were official agents of the U.S. Government.

They played a key role in sabotaging the Egyptian Army so that the Jews won their first great victory in 1948. Now the infant nation, established by bandits, had the world's most expensive espionage network, the CIA, whose budget was paid entirely by the American taxpayer, three hundred million dollars a year. Now, in 1968, it is $1,500,000,000 a year.

GENTILE FRONT

As the new Elmer Davis, the Jews again found a gentile who could be manipulated as a stool pigeon for Israel. This was Allen Dulles, who, after an ineffectual career as a bond peddler, had existed as a pale shadow of his brother, John Foster Dulles. A partner in the firm of Sullivan and Cromwell, Wall Street lawyers for the leading international Jewish bankers, John Foster Dulles had enabled the Jews to bring off many financial coups which impoverished gentile Americans. Now his brother became the front behind which Israeli intelligence agents scored their greatest success through the CIA. The network was "blown" for a time in 1949, when Dr. Warren Spock, an economist, exposed the fact that the CIA had set up a fifty-million-dollar fund in a Swiss Bank which was available only to Israeli agents. Dulles defended the arrangement by saying that the Israelis were the best spies in the world and were cheap at the price. The arrangement was continued by the CIA.

REVOLUTION IN LATIN AMERICA

Although their primary function was espionage for Israel, the CIA also devoted much of its efforts to. overthrowing anti-Communist governments in Latin America. The first target was Argentina. A family of German Jews, the Bambergs, had stolen rayon patents in Europe and established textile factories in Argentina. They amassed a two-billion-dollar fortune without paying a cent of taxes, due to their bribery of tax officials in Argentina. When Juan Peron came to power in Argentina through the efforts of white Christian Argentine workers, he found that the Jews controlled all of the nation's commerce, due to phony tax deals. He fired the corrupt officials, and as a start, he levied back taxes of one hundred and fifty million dollars against the Bambergs. They immediately turned to world Jewry for their defence, and they launched an international propaganda campaign against Peron unequalled for vileness. Then the CIA was called in.

MASQUERADE AS PRIESTS

Fifty CIA agents were sent to Buenos Aires, where, in the garb of Catholic priests, they directed a revolution against Peron. Even the Catholic Peron believed that the Vatican had turned against him, and the Catholic population obeyed the priests and revolted against him. The Bamberg fortune was safe. Frei and a motley crew of Jews took over the government, and pushed Argentina into bankruptcy, so that the Jews seized all assets of the nation.

Peron had also been known as staunchly opposed to Communism, and the defeat of this Christian leader impelled the CIA to go after other Latin American leaders who were known as anti-Communist. Jiminez of Venezuela was the next to fall, and when he came to the United States as a refugee, our government returned him to Venezuela to be imprisoned on trumped-up charges, unlike the Jewish refugees who, when they fled criminal charges, were always welcomed to our shores. Now the Communists were free to burn and pillage American businesses in Venezuela, and a state of revolution has existed ever since the CIA overthrew Jiminez.

BATISTA

Under Fulgencia Batista's enlightened rule, Cuba enjoyed the highest standard of living in Latin America. However, he was also known as a fierce opponent of Communism. The CIA spent many millions to finance Fidel Castro's revolution, while they directed an American propaganda campaign against Batista's "fascist" rule. Fascism, of course, simply means "anti-Communism". Most of the CIA material was surfaced through the New York Times, a CIA organ, with one journalist, Herbert Matthews, stationed with the Castro forces. Matthews assured the American people that Castro was not a Communist, although Castro later boasted that he had been a Communist for twenty years.

COUNTER-REVOLUTION

After the brutal Communist dictatorship of Castro had horrified the world with its mass executions a la Leon Trotsky, ninety per cent of the Cuban people were ready to risk their lives to overthrow him. Once again, he turned to the CIA for help. CIA agents were rushed to Cuba, circulating among the people and taking the names of anti-Communists. The leaders were then arrested and killed. The rest were told to take no action until the CIA landed a liberation army. The liberation army was organized and trained by the CIA, with daily information sent to Castro of its strength and plans. Some of the officers of this army, who were members of Cuba's oldest Christian families, learned of the CIA treachery when they overheard CIA radio transmissions to Havana from the training camp. They were murdered and their bodies thrown over a cliff. The others were assured of air cover when they staged their landing, but when they landed, zeroed in by the Castro forces, no planes appeared, and they were massacred, in another typical CIA horror. The survivors were herded into bestial prisons.

Meanwhile, the shattered economy of Cuba, under Communist dictatorship, was unable to produce such necessities as medicines. Once again, the CIA rushed to Castro's rescue. They suggested that he "ransom" the surviving freedom fighters in exchange for many tons of needed medicines, and again the tottering Castro regime was saved. This ransom of victims was the most shameful episode in American history, since we bartered with a savage Communist mercenary and paid his blackmail to save his own skin. As usual, Robert F. Kennedy played a front role in this sordid transaction, a new low of human degradation.

Now the CIA organized a Castro front in America, known as the Fair Play for Cuba Committee, whose New Orleans manager was Lee Harvey Oswald.

HUNGARIAN ATROCITY

One of the CIA's principal functions has been to expose, misdirect, and annihilate anti-Communist movements all over the world. In 1956, one of the most potent of these groups threatened the continued Soviet dictatorship in Hungary. At the same time, Israel had conspired with England and France to launch a blitzkrieg attack to wipe out Egypt. A diversion was necessary to prevent world opinion from turning against the Jewish bandits, Once again, the CIA came up with the answer. At the moment the Jews launched their sneak attack, the CIA would sponsor an anti-Communist uprising in Hungary. The eyes of the world would be upon Hungary, while the Voice of America broadcast to the Hungarians that American help would be arriving soon. Meanwhile, Israel, with the aid of the French Air Force and the British Army, would wipe out Egypt and become the master of the Middle East.

Eisenhower, who was known throughout Europe as "the mad Butcher of Berlin" because of his massacres of German families in that city, and who turned over thousands of Russian freedom fighters to he executed by the Red Army firing squads, once again was true to his role. He cheered on the Hungarian patriots to their deaths, while Russian tanks slaughtered them as they stared at the skies for the American help which never came. Meanwhile, the Egyptian Army held firm, and the

Eden government in England was dismissed because of this shameful episode on behalf of Israel. The Jewish bandits retired to await a more favourable moment for attack, and the anti-Communist movement in Hungary was wiped out. Once again, the CIA had achieved two aims with one manoeuvre. Satan had won again.

CIA PERSONNEL

Capitol Hill observers consider the CIA to be made up of three groups, alcoholics at the top, sexual degenerates, and Communists. Some executives fall into all three categories, others fit into one or more. One executive deposits five thousand dollars a month in a Swiss Bank, payments from the Soviet Fourth Bureau. Another, who squirrelled away enormous sums in the past five years, had his "suicide" arranged by CIA colleagues who felt themselves short-changed.

The CIA administers lie detector tests to prospective employees, in order to establish the degree of sexual deviation. The purpose of this is to measure the deviate's attitude towards his own degeneracy. If he is cool and arrogant about it, the CIA immediately hires him, because they know that hardened deviates make the best killers, a fact long known to the Mafia. If he is nervous and guilty about it, the CIA refuses to employ him, because he will be of no use to them.

ORIGIN OF THE FBI

Shortly after World War I, American patriots in Congress urged the formation of a department to control widespread Communist espionage. It began under the direction of two well-known anti-Communists who had an unparalleled background of study of this movement. After some mouths, during which they achieved a great deal in laying the groundwork for control of Communist subversion, they were suddenly dismissed, and a protege of the left-wing Judge, Harlan Stone, was placed in charge of this department, which became known as the Federal Bureau of Investigation.

This epigone was a sallow-faced, unhealthily plump young man named J. Edgar Hoover. Kinky-haired and bulging-eyed, he was of uncertain origins, but with his powerful backing, the FBI gained in power and prestige each year. So, amazingly enough, did the forces of organized crime and organized Communist subversion in America!

SURVIVOR

J. Edgar Hoover is unique among secret police chiefs in the twentieth century, in that he has survived. Himmler, Yagoda and Beria died violently, but Hoover bears a charmed life. Why is this? Why did Lyndon B. Johnson enact legislation to keep J. Edgar Hoover in power for life? The answer is that J. Edgar Hoover is a master diplomat, who has always made secret treaties with those who would be interested in seeing him dead, that is, his ostensible enemies, the Mafia and the Communist Party. The Mafia could not operate for a single day without the active cooperation of officials in all levels of the government, because adequate legislation exists to control them, Arlen Spector, District Attorney of Philadelphia, recently said, "The Mafia levies taxes against American citizens as 'protection money'. It also passes death sentences against American citizens who break its laws. Thus it has, by armed force, usurped the functions of the United States Government, and any member of this organization, or anyone giving aid and comfort to it, is in armed insurrection against the government, and subject to arrest and execution." Mayor John Lindsay of New York echoed this sentiment when he said, "The gang members of the Mafia, who comprise an armed revolt against the American people, should he made subject to the death penalty, even as they have sentenced and executed thousands of American citizens for disobeying their laws."

TILE "ITALIAN" MAFIA

One of the great triumphs of the American journalists has been the legend that organized crime is Italian, a group of Sicilian hoods. In reality, the boss of the Mafia is the Jew,

Meyer Lansky, and the Sicilians are only the enforcement arm of the Syndicate, which is sixty per cent Jewish. In the early 1920s, crime consisted of small groups of Jewish, Italian and Irish gangsters in the cities of New York, Chicago, and Philadelphia. The Italians began a war of extermination against the Irish hoods, and killed off most of them. Public opinion was aroused by these gangland massacres, and Meyer Lansky called in the Sicilians, persuaded them to form a business combine, and used them as a collection agency for Jewish bookmakers, while Lansky and his Jewish henchman, Longie Zwillman, ran the national Syndicate. Moe Annenberg handled all communications for the Syndicate.

The Mafia has also been the political enforcement arm for the Democratic Party. It was the Sicilian gangsters who delivered the Chicago vote for John F. Kennedy and swung the close election to the Democrats in 1960. Soon afterwards, the Dept. of Justice began a frantic effort to convince the American public that the Syndicate was Italian, through the revelations of a small-time hoodlum named Joseph Valachi. Since anyone who knew anything about crime knew that sixty per cent of the Syndicate was Jewish, this frenetic effort was largely wasted. Lansky is still the Boss of the Syndicate.

HATES NEGROES

It is known in Washington that J. Edgar Hoover has hated

and feared Negroes all of his life. There are two current explanations among Capitol Hill insiders. One is that Hoover is "passing", and exhibits the characteristics of this type. The other is that Hoover was molested by a Negro handyman when he was ten years old, and that this occurrence not only gave him a strange attitude towards physical sex, but also engendered a fierce hatred of Negroes. For many years, under his orders, the FBI refused to employ any Negro except as janitor or elevator man. There were no Negro FBI agents, administrative employees, or secretaries. In 1939, Eleanor Roosevelt sent a light-skinned Negro girl, an intimate friend, to work at the FBI as a secretary. For three days she sat in an office, and was not given anything to do, while no one dared to speak to her. Finally, she burst into tears and went home, never to return.

Several Washington wits commented that this type of anti-Negro feeling is common among those of grey skin, bulging eyes, and kinky hair, such as J. Edgar Hoover. At any rate, no one has ever been able to pinpoint his racial origins.

Despite his hatred of Negroes, J, Edgar Hoover was forced to employ the entire force of FBI agents against the American people to aid Marxist-led, Moscow-trained Negro revolutionists in outbreaks of armed violence, while the Mafia operated unmolested. This odd turn of events came about because of the Presidential aspirations of Richard Nixon. Always playing it safe and losing everything, Nixon decided that even though he was the heir apparent to the Eisenhower throne, he needed to hedge his bets. His Jewish advisor, Chotiner, a representative of Syndicate interests, urged him to make a play for the Negro vote, and he asked his closest friend, Attorney General William Rogers, to enlist the FBI as a task force to implement the Negro revolution against white citizens. Rogers was the latest in a long line of political nobodies chosen as Attorney General solely because they would not object to any government outrage against human decency and the American people.

HOOVER SWALLOWS HIS PRIDE

Although J. Edgar Hoover was chagrined at ordering his agents to become the emissaries of Black Power, as usual, he swallowed his pride and obeyed orders. Like all bureaucrats, he despised the working people, and be saw in this order a new opportunity to violate every civil right of the American white workers. He sent regiments of FBI agents to small Southern towns, in many cases outnumbering the inhabitants, to enforce brutal decrees against the white citizens. When three professional agitators disappeared in Mississippi, J. Edgar Hoover dispatched 347 FBI agents to a town of 200 people. The same day, four white people were stabbed to death by black thugs in New York City subways, and the Mafia continued to operate unmolested throughout the country. The government spent thirty millions of dollars in the search for the agitators, and the FBI paid one informer $75,000 in cash.

FBI REIGN OF TERROR

Many white Americans who opposed. the Black Revolution had their homes forcibly entered by FBI agents, their telephones tapped, their personal papers stolen, white FBI agents forced their employers to discharge them without notice. Eleven white people are known to have died as the direct result of this FBI reign of terror.

REMODELING THE SYNAGOGUES

In Atlanta, Georgia, a rabbi wished to remodel his synagogue, but he could not raise the funds. A local FBI informer arranged for a wall to be blown out where the rooms were to be added, and evidence against five local patriots was planted by the FBI, while the FBI informer appeared as the only witness against them. Twenty million dollars was raised through a national propaganda campaign, to rebuild the "shattered" synagogue, and although Georgia law enforcement officials possess evidence that the FBI informer was the only perpetrator of this outrage, he has never been prosecuted. The case against the five patriots was dismissed.

Because of many such instances, Americans realize that the FBI is a joke in the area of law enforcement. The famous list of the Ten Most Wanted Criminals contains such anomalies as yokels wanted for wife-beating or check forgery, but no Mafia gang official has ever been listed as one of the Ten Most Wanted men. J. Edgar Hoover persuaded Hollywood Jews to make a number of movies glorifying the FBI, and a television series was begun, which has run at a loss ever since it was inaugurated. None of this helped the dimming image of the FBI, while the growing power of crime and Communism in America convinced everyone that the FBI was either ineffectual or in open connivance with traitors and criminals.

HOOVER A FRONT MAN

Only a half dozen people in Washington know that in 1953 J. Edgar Hoover was relieved as Director of the FBI. Although he continued to hold the office, and the title, control of the FBI passed to a Jew from Hong Kong named David Liberman, who had been a protege of the Communist leader Bukharin. Liberman entered the United States in 1932, and later went to the Department of Agriculture under Henry Wallace. He was employed in the name of D. Thomas Lee, and he set up four Communist networks in Washington, none of which know the members of the others. In 1939 he was shifted to the FBI, where he was given charge of a department specializing in planting phony evidence against loyal German-Americans so that they could be imprisoned and their homes and businesses given to Jews. He now operated under the cover name of Hawkins, and it is this name which he used today as the secret director of the FBI. A graduate of the Lenin School of Revolution in Moscow, he trained the group which later delivered China to the Communists. Interestingly enough, when Robert F. Kennedy, as Attorney General, was in nominal charge of the FBI, he dealt only with J. Edgar Hoover, and was unaware of Hawkins' existence.

THE KENNEDY MYTH

Of all groups with the capacity to do evil, and to advance the work of Satan, none exceeds the journalists. The profession of journalism as we know it was developed by the Rothschilds in France after they won power in that unfortunate country. Operating on their well-known theory that everything and everyone was for sale, the Rothschilds used the press as a means for buying and selling, and this it has remained. When they wished to sell something, the press played it up as a great bargain. When they wished to buy, the press attacked their objective and drove its price to rock bottom.

Although the publishers were the only people who mattered, clerks were hired to write up the stories, and the nearly illiterate flotsam and jetsam which comprised this group soon began to think of themselves as world movers. From its inception, journalism was always a gutter occupation, and the more persuasive they are, the higher price the journalists command. When they demand too much, they are easily replaced from the lowest segments of humanity, for they share a common venality and lack of all principle.

The journalists have learned how to create gods from mere mortals, or so they describe their efforts. Their most successful achievement was the Kennedy myth, whereby a pleasant-faced, wealthy young man of little accomplishments was transformed into a world figure. His father, Joseph Kennedy, is known as the most ruthless businessman in America. WIC was once asked the essential ingredients for making a fortune. He candidly replied, "Luck and greed."

THE GREAT AMERICAN PHONIES

Joseph Kennedy's sons became public figures as the products of advertising, that is, by spending money to put over a product. A sick man, John F. Kennedy turned the White House over to the group of clever Jews who had helped him to win that objective. Despite their vast wealth, and their reputation as connoisseurs of arts, the Kennedys buy no paintings or sculpture, and have never been known to aid an artist. Their homes are examples of typical nouveau riche, Better Homes and Gardens decor.

Because of their insincere treatment of artists, the Kennedys were amazed when many invited artists refused to attend the inauguration. Only a few pathetic has-beens, such as Robert Frost, greedily seized upon the opportunity for self-publicizing. The Kennedys put an end to their dream when they agreed to the demands of their sneering left wing Jewish cohorts that they dump Lyndon Johnson in 1964. The fact was that Johnson commanded more political muscle than JFK. Also, he bitterly hated JFK for having been able to purchase the White House with a campaign which Johnson had been unable to afford.

THE STALIN-TROTSKY IMPASSE

A situation now developed like that between Stalin and Trotsky in Russia in the 1920's. Like Trotsky, JFK led a pack of hysterical Jewish Marxist demagogues, and like Lyndon Johnson led a well-organized and obedient group of careerists. The outcome could not be in doubt to anyone who knew the result of the Stalin-Trotsky imbroglio. The opposing forces were drawn up behind the shock troops of the FBI, for John F. Kennedy, and the CIA, for Johnson. Johnson's forces included some eager, half-educated, but tough young men, who were homosexuals, and these perverts had established close relationships with homosexuals in commanding positions of the CIA. Also, Johnson was responsible for pushing through, as Senate Majority Leader, the enormous appropriations for the CIA, which amounted to fifty times the amount budgeted for the FBI. Thus, in this struggle, the tables were turned, for instead of Kennedy having unlimited funds to advance his cause, it was now Johnson who could devote the enormous budget of the CIA for his own career.

Despite the fact that in this power struggle, Kennedy seemingly had much greater resources than Johnson, as Commander-in-Chief of the armed forces, and with the huge forces of the Executive Department, as well as his brother Bobby. the Attorney General, in charge of the FBI, in fact, as the outcome showed, John F. Kennedy really led none of his forces, but, rather, was used by them, whereas Johnson was in absolute command of every resource beholden to him.

Haying obtained Kennedy's promise to dump Johnson iii 1964, the Jewish Marxist demagogues sat back, convinced that they had won, when in fact, the struggle had not yet begun. Johnson had no intention of returning to Texas and sitting on his front porch for thirty years as John Garner had done. At the very moment that Kennedy was in greatest danger, his brother Bobby had, through a series of blunders, alienated the only man who could have saved him, J. Edgar Hoover.

Previous Attorney Generals had been weak political hacks who feared Hoover and never interfered with him. Bobby Kennedy was the first Attorney General who was wealthy in his own right, and who was a power in the White House. Now Bobby's Jewish advisers urged him to attack Hoover on one of his sacred grounds, the exclusion of Negroes as FBI agents. Bobby ordered J. Edgar Hoover to appoint twenty-five Negro FBI agents within two weeks. A month passed, and none were appointed. Bobby stormed into Hoover's office, and a furious scene took place in the sanctum which no previous Attorney General had dared to enter without permission. Bobby's next move was to challenge Hoover on the seeming immunity of the Mafia from FBI interference. A Jew named Everett Glass, also known as Mervin MacArthur and O. Klein, had claimed that on Sept. 2, 1938, the Mafia and the FBI had made a Concordat whereby the Mafia would apprehend non-Mafia offenders throughout the United States, and the FBI would not interfere in any Mafia operation. These negotiations were the result of the Mafia's repeated gestures of goodwill, such as a Mafia informer tipping off the FBI to John Dillinger's presence in the Biograph Theatre in Chicago, so that the courageous FBI men could machine gun down the Public Enemy Number One from concealed positions as he emerged from a quiet evening at the movies.

Glass also claimed, shortly before his nude corpse was found stuffed into a sewer opening, that two FBI agents were appointed to carry out assassinations for the Mafia, relieving the Mafia hoods from the danger of carrying guns. The two agents who assumed this duty were known only by numbers, not by names, and when Ian Fleming, a

British writer, visited in Washington, highly-placed friends mentioned the strange duties of this pair. Fleming used the revelation to invent a series about a British agent, known only by number, who was licensed to kill, and so James Bond, Secret Agent 007, was born.

Three weeks before Kennedy's assassination, Bobby Kennedy put J. Edgar Hoover in an untenable position by declaring war upon the Mafia, authorizing special task forces, ordering unlimited wire-tapping, and other means of apprehension, Thus, at a critical moment, the FBI support was alienated. Despite the fact that Hoover had infiltrated the CIA with his personal informers, nothing was said about the rifle team which was dispatched to Dallas the day before Kennedy was scheduled to appear there. After the assassination, Johnson passed a special act allowing J. Edgar Hoover to remain in command of the FBI for life. No one has ever accused LBJ of ingratitude.

The chief of Scotland Yard, when queried about the assassination, said, "A detective always looks for the motive. Of course there was only one person in the world who stood to benefit from Kennedy's death." In an early edition soon after the assassination, the New York Times reported a rumour that Kennedy had been murdered because of a dispute between two contending groups of homosexuals in Washington, but this edition disappeared from the stands in a few minutes.

John F. Kennedy had been lured to Dallas by the one thing

which his advisers wanted to hear, a confession of weakness from "Anson, who claimed his following in Texas was shaky, and that he needed Kennedy's aid with a personal appearance. They urged Kennedy to accept, because this would give him a logical excuse for a later announcement that he had to dump Johnson because he couldn't carry his own state.

GARRISON

When the District Attorney of New Orleans, Jim Garrison, broke the news of the CIA plot, the CIA prepared a one-hour "news special" for CBS which was an abortive attempt to discredit him, and which demonstrated the Jewish use of TV for partisan purposes.

The death of his brother broke Robert F. Kennedy's spirit. His father had never warned him that people on Capitol Hill play with marked cards, or that even a great fortune will not last forever in a crooked game. He became a Charlie McCarthy, still young, still bright, still mouthing the pat Marxist phrases of his Jewish advisers, but in his appearances, the audience was uneasily aware that although the dummy still held their interest, they were disturbed by the absence of the ventriloquist. The monarchy envisioned by a greed old man has already vanished into the land of might-have-been in which the Roosevelt sons have existed since 1945.

THE KATZENBACISTS

Because of the total perversion of communications by the Jews, Americans now have an accurate guide to good and evil. Whatever is praised in the press, and on radio and TV, is most assuredly the work of the Devil, while anything that is attacked by these media is in Christ. This total perversion was achieved through racism, a furious Jewish racism which attacked and subverted all other racial groups in America. The principal agents of the Jews in this perversion are a hybrid racial group of mulattoes known as "Katzenbachists".

What is the origin of the Katzenbachists? During the early 1800's, Baron James de Rothschild of Paris employed an American turncoat, Nicholas Biddle, to set up a Bank of the United States which would become the vehicle of Rothschild power over America. A great patriot, General Andrew Jackson, discovered the plot, and thwarted it. The Rothschilds looked for another way to subdue America.

SLAVES

Yankee entrepreneurs had brought slaves to America, but they were unable to work well in the harsh Northern climate, and most of them were unloaded on Southern planters at enormous profits. Once the Yankees had saturated the South with inefficient and expensive black labour, they complained that slavery was evil and unjust.

The Rothschilds seized upon this opening, and poured millions of dollars into New England to finance anti-slavery movements. The Abolitionists operated with religious fervour, stealing slaves and bringing them North. So fanatical were they that the Abolitionist Yankees gave their daughters to the runaway slaves in marriage, creating a mulatto class from rundown, mentally unbalanced New England white stock and healthy black flesh.

Because these were prominent families, by the close of the Civil War, the mulattoes were being given prominent positions in education, the church, and government. At the same time, the Rothschilds created fortunes for them by investing in railroad stocks through the firms of Kuhn, Loeb Co., and J. P. Morgan Co. This the grey-skinned, bulging-eyed, thick-lipped and prematurely-balding mulatto ruling class not only assumed leadership in many fields, but also had great fortunes at their command.

Meanwhile, the Jewish hankers created panic after panic, in 1893, 1907, and 1929, in which the gentile white middle class was systematically impoverished. The Crash of 1929 left the mulatto aristocracy and their Jewish overlords in full command of white America. The mulatto university presidents hired lisping Yiddish Communists from Russia, such as Kerensky, in all of our famous schools, and fired the white professors. Mulatto government officials carried on a furious campaign against all white patriots, imprisoning them on false evidence, destroying their businesses, and ruining their families.

One of the mulattoes, a president of Harvard, remarked that the Constitution wasn't even useful as toilet paper anymore. Mulatto judges ruled against any white person brought before them, committing many of them to sordid asylums as "mentally ill". White cities, built by white labour, were turned over to Negro hordes as the white people were systematically driven from their homes. Mulatto bankers foreclosed all mortgages held by white investors.

Now, all of this is known to Americans, but they do not resist. Why is this? Because they have abandoned Christ, and this they will lose everything. We know that the centre of power of the mulatto aristocracy and the Jewish overlords is the Council on Foreign Relations, we know that all government departments, schools, churches and banks are devoted to extending mulatto and Jewish power over white American workers who are the toiling slaves of this system. How can we save ourselves? By living in Christ.

There is nothing complicated about the cosmogony of good and evil. Every American knows that men prominent in public life are intent upon our destruction, but we have lost our honour, we are ashamed to show ourselves to Christ as the miserable, degraded slaves of the mulatto aristocracy which we have become. But we are miserable and degraded only because we are not living in Christ. The power of the Devil, our supine existence in Satan's Empire, is precisely why we need Christ.

Now it is time for white Americans to take the long road back, to save themselves and the world from the approaching self-destruction of Satan's Empire. We know the situation. We know that every newspaper, every television station, every school, bank and museum is an agent of the Devil. Our enemies strut before us, unconcealed, arrogant in the attire of Satan. Only by opposing them, by giving yourself to this struggle, can you know Christ and become serene in His love. The decision is yours alone; to remain the wretched thing that you are, a willing slave of the mulatto aristocracy and the Jewish overlords, or to rise to glory in the arms of Jesus.

OPEN WAR

The Secretary of State, Dean Husk, spoke frankly, calling a spade a spade, when he told reporters, "This is the proudest moment of my life," The occasion was his giving his daughter to a black boy from Washington in a new trend towards interracial marriages among the ruling class. Many Americans wondered about this strange perversion of values, without understanding that the bulging-eyed, gray-skinned, balding mulatto aristocrat has one burning characteristic, a hatred of the white race, to which he can never really belong, and a sense of rejection by the black race, which ridicules him as a bastard and a hybrid. This explains the mulatto's furious war against the white race, which he holds responsible for his uncomfortable predicament. This is why church leaders, educators and government officials do everything in their power to injure white Americans. This is why the worst poverty in America today is in Appalachia, the birthplace of the American Republic and the home of white pioneers. Native-born white Americans have been reduced to the most abject poverty, while the government pours billions of dollars into Negro city slums to enable Negroes to live without working.

When white American sailors are massacred by Israeli planes in a sneak attack on the U.S. Liberty, the mulatto aristocracy in America cheers the attackers. Our government wages a propaganda war against a few small white nations whose crime is that they have white governments. Having declared their independence from England, in following America's tradition, white Rhodesians were stunned to find the American government urging England to make war against them! The Union of South Africa patiently endures provocative acts by our mulatto government, while the American press carries on an unprecedented hate campaign against them. The furious hate campaign against these white nations reveals to the world that the American government is an anti-white government.

WHITE REPRESSION

In the United States, white citizens are subjected to repressions which make the Soviet Union seem a Promised Land of Freedom. Descendants of the white founders of America languish in Appalachia, in tragic and hopeless poverty, while white citizens who have been more fortunate find that every agency of the mulatto government attempts to rob them of their income, and conducts a ruthless campaign to force all white homes, schools and clubs to open their doors to black aggressors.

EQUAL JUSTICE UNDER LAW

Under this proud motto, the Supreme Court of the United States has led the way in dispensing unequal justice for the past fifty years. White citizens are dispossessed and disenfranchised by court decisions. Income tax laws are not enforced against Negroes. Joe Louis owed one million dollars in back taxes which was waived, Adam Clayton Powell defied the government to prosecute him, and they dropped the case, although millions of dollars had flowed through his hands in government funds, with no accounting made.

A white citizen, John Kasper, suggested that the citizens

of Clinton, Tennessee, use the right of petition to redress a Constitutional grievance, the illegal and forced integration of local schools. A Federal judge promptly sentenced him to a year in jail, and later he was given another year's sentence on a similar charge. In contrast, the Black Power leader, H. Rap Brown, urges Negro mobs to burn down cities, and the government frees him, against the smoking ruins of Cambridge, Watts, Rochester, Chicago, and Detroit.

THE "BLACK" REVOLUTION IN AMERICA

As we have seen, the so-called "Black Revolution" is not black in its origins, nor is it a revolution. It is merely a successful power play by the mulatto aristocrats and their Jewish overlords in America.

What is a revolution? In the history books, the student will not find the definition of a revolution which is presented here for the first time. A revolution is a political event in which people are used. Trotsky complained that "Every revolution is betrayed". But it is not the revolution which is betrayed. The people are betrayed. They are used, just as the mulatto aristocrats are using the American Negro community as a pawn in their power play, which they camouflage under the name of the "Black Revolution."

A large part of the national income is being diverted to

the Black Revolution, as the government plans to spend thirty-five BILLION dollars in cash for the Poverty Program. Think of that, thirty-five billion dollars in slush funds to be used as a weapon against white Americans! Successful revolutions have been achieved with a few million dollars in modern times, although Jacob Schiff of Kuhn, Loeb Co. in New York had to spend twenty-five millions of Rothschild money to bring about the Bolshevik Revolution in Russia. Now the Marxist revolutionaries have thirty-five billions to use against the American people.

The white poor, who make up the majority of low income citizens of America, will receive none of the Poverty Funds. It is all earmarked for Black Power, to pay an army of Marxist revolutionaries to swarm over America, crushing local and state governments with the power of the public purse. The future of America lies in this thirty-five billion dollar Poverty Fund, but the white citizens do not realize what is going on, they do not know they are to be destroyed. Meanwhile, the Federal government releases a study of the riots of 1965, 1966, and 1967 in which black mobs burned down many American cities. The study claims that the riots were due to "white racism", a completely insane conclusion. The study recommends making war on white citizens, in order to discourage black citizens from burning down more cities.

CHAPTER THREE

HOW I CAME TO CHRIST

IN 1955, one of the great ladies of the American patriotic movement, Mrs. Lyrl Clark Van Hyning, publisher of the fearless newspaper, Women's Voice, in Chicago, listened to a hysterical denunciation of me from an agent provocateur of the Jewish espionage group, the Anti- Defamation League. He had come from New York to prevent us from working together, and he informed her that I was a dangerous, armed criminal who lived by robbing banks. Mrs. an Hyning listened to these falsehoods, and replied, "Eustace Mullins has paid the price. That is why he can do so much in this work.'

When this story was relayed to me by one who was present, I was mildly surprised. It had never occurred to me that I was "paying a price". It was true that I had lost everything the average American holds dear, money, a career, and social position. At the age of thirty-two, I had been working ten years an average of eighteen hours a day, studying, writing, and lecturing on the dangers of Communism and during those years, I had earned four thousand dollars, an average of four hundred dollars a year. I had never owned any property, not even an automobile, which the poorest Negro can acquire in this country.

I had been discharged from one promising position after another, at the active instigation of the ADL and the FBI. I had been hounded from one city to another, my family had been turned against me, but it had not occurred to me that I was making a sacrifice, nor did I realize that I was working for Christ. Like most young people, I was disgusted by the treason and corruption apparent at every level of American life. When I went to Washington in 1948, the moral stench of the pitiful wretches in the White House and on Capitol Hill had turned my stomach. I naively supposed that no decent American wished to live in a sewer, and I did what I could to turn the tide.

A BEGINNING

On my arrival in Washington, as a Virginian of good family, I was well-received in the upper levels of society, and I became the protege of several of the most respected people in the city. As a young poet of no particular political allegiance, and of some promise, I found many doors opened for me. Luther Evans, the Librarian of Congress, personally invited me to join the staff, and in six months, I received three promotions and many commendations before I was suddenly discharged. What had happened?

A friend had asked me to accompany him to visit an inmate of St. Elizabeth's Hospital in Washington. He confided that the inmate, a poet named Ezra Pound, was a political prisoner. I had no reaction one way or another, until I was ushered into the corner of the ward in which the prisoner sat with his wife. When he looked at me, f was immediately overcome with tremendous anger. The kind gaze of a great gentleman informed me that I was living in a nation which had condemned one of its important minds to a living hell. Our initial conversation was that of people who had known each other for many years. He asked nothing of me, but that look had asked everything. When I left the hospital that day, I had crossed the Rubicon.

I plunged into a study of the Federal Reserve System, at Pound's suggestion. The nature of my work at the Library gave me access to every area, and I found whole shelves of books which were not listed in the catalogue. Others, marked as Missing, had been shoved down behind the stacks. From these books I made thousands of pages of notes, photocopying many of them, while no one paid any attention to me, for it was well known that I had been hired by the Librarian himself.

These notes *formed the basis of the books, "Mullins on the Federal Reserve," "The History of the Jews,", "This Difficult Individual, Ezra Pound,"* among my published works, as well as four manuscripts not yet published.

These were days of great excitement for me. I had discovered the nature of the world in which I lived. Without telling Pound, I published some of my findings in a small, patriotic newsletter. A few days later, Senator Herbert Lehman, national chairman of the Anti-Defamation League, called Luther Evans and told him I must be fired immediately. It was a shattering blow for Evans, who immediately reached for the second drawer of his desk, in which he kept his daily fifth of nerve medicine.

Ezra was quite annoyed with me. "Didn't I tell you I've always been too reckless?" he demanded. "At least try to stay out of jail, it's too great a limitation on your activities."

I did not try to justify myself by explaining that when I saw him imprisoned in a madhouse by the madmen who had seized control of our country, I could not restrain myself. It was useless to claim that a penniless youth from the backwoods had a chance to overthrow the insane international Jewish bankers who pulled the strings of the perverted puppets in Washington. And yet, even then, unconsciously, I knew that anything was possible in Christ, of Whom I was not even aware. I had no way of knowing that the putrescent cloud of evil which had darkened our lives was, according to the laws of physics, the most vulnerable at the time of its greatest expansion.

FIRST BLOOD

I drew first blood from the enemy with the publication of *"Mullins on the Federal Reserve"'*, in April, 1952. The book had been completed in 1950, and had been rejected by every New York publishing house, with varying excuses, and ignoring the fact that no history of the Federal Reserve System had ever been published. A young man, John Kasper, borrowed money from a lady to finance a small edition, and the lady's husband divorced her because of this, but the book was on its way. It created a tremendous impact, and an official of the Bank of America agreed to back an edition of 100,000 hard cover copies, until pressure was brought to bear upon him by the Treasury Department, and the agreement was cancelled.

Late in 1953, a man who published a small patriotic newsletter informed me that he had a commission from a wealthy automobile manufacturer to publish ten thousand copies of the book, which were to be sent to every judge, and every federal and state legislature in the United States. I was greatly pleased by this development, and I generously agreed to waive royalties on the ten thousand copies, in order to give even more money for mailing the books first class.

I had no way of knowing that this man was a front for a Jew who had founded the Anti-Defamation League, or that his newspaper was held in the name of a Jewish provocateur for the ADL, or that the purpose of this newspaper was to subvert, confound and destroy every patriotic organization which fell into its influence. It succeeded, during the next ten years, in exterminating every anti-Communist group in the New York area, and the ADL financed its work with the income from my book, of which it sold 200,000 copies during the next twelve years, without my being able to collect a cent in royalties, although my waiver had only covered the initial ten thousand copies, published as "***The Federal Reserve Conspiracy***".

Not only this, but another self-styled patriot copied the name, the format and exact appearance of my hook, and sold 60,000 copies during the next ten years. Then another "patriot" published a book on the Federal Reserve, and boldly plagiarized three entire chapters. Both plagiarists are selling widely today.

Despite the fact that I had collected nothing, and that the ADL had held firm to its decision in 1952 that "Mullins will never have a cent as long as he lives," a decision which was reported to me from an unimpeachable source, my book's circulation in Washington averted two major depressions in the next ten years, The Jews dared not use the Federal Reserve Board for another abrupt contraction of credit to impoverish the white workers, because I had exposed their classic techniques in my book. I asked for no thanks, and received none.

A BUSY LIFE

I was too busy to think about money. I had hosts of friends, many of them well-to-do, and although I never saw any cash, I lived well as a guest in many fine homes, while I continued my work. No sooner had I been fired from the Library of Congress than friendly legislators used my information to on an investigation of the appalling mal-administration of the Library. Luther Evans resigned and fled to Paris, where he remained for years as a pensioner of UNESCO, at a handsome salary.

I COME TO MCCARTHY'S AID

At this time, Senator Joe McCarthy needed much assistance from the Legislative Reference Service of the Library of Congress. Pro-Communists in this department deliberately fed him wrong information, in order to discredit his exposures of Communists in the Truman Administration, the Hisses, Chambers and many others who had dug in while undermining all of the institutions of America life, I was asked to become his special legislative assistant for research, and for some months I played an important rose in the Benton episode and other McCarthy battles, At this time, because of national alarm over McCarthy's exposure of Communist subversion, his office expenses were exceeding his salary by $20,000 a month, as he tried to keep tip with his mail. Unlike other

Senators, he had no millions of his own and no private sources of graft to pay his bills. Knowing of leis problems, George Sokolsky asked him to lunch in Georgetown, and told him that it was necessary for the Jews to take over his exposure of Communists, because ninety per cent of the people he had named as spies were Jewish. When McCarthy refused, Sokolsky set up a lunch for him at the Carlyle Hotel, in New York City, with Bernard Baruch. McCarthy emerged from this meeting visibly shaken, because Baruch had warned him he had two weeks to turn over his anti-Communist crusade to the Jews, or he would be assassinated.

THE COHN AND SCHINE CIRCUS

McCarthy accepted a $50,000 advance payment to clear up his outstanding office bills, and two arrogant young Jews took over his office. Roy Cohn was the son of an ADL chieftain in New York, one of the most sinister figures in this Gestapo organization of furtive conspirators who were repeatedly denounced by Westbrook Pegler and other patriots.

David Schine was the son of J. Myer Schine, whom Middletown, N.Y., residents remember as an itinerant peddler walking the roads with a pack on his back. He began to show lantern slides in barns, and at this time, Jewish gangsters in New York were financing Jewish couples from Brooklyn to open resort hotels in the

Catskills which the hoods could use as hideouts, with ponds and lakes in which the bodies of their victims could be sunk. This resulted in the network of expensive hotels which later earned this area the nickname of the Jewish Alps", financed by Murder, Inc.

J. Elver Schine was backed in a chain of movie houses and hotels, including the Roney Plaza Hotel in Miami Beach, which became the official winter headquarters of the Syndicate. This five hundred-million-dollar empire produced the revenue which purchased McCarthy's office for the Jews. They effectively castrated McCarthy's campaign against Communism, and sent him, a tragic figure in those last months, to his death. At any rate, I had been the first on whom the ADL axe fell when they took over McCarthy's office, and although many of his supporters wrote indignantly to him about my discharge, he never once replied to them.

THE NEW YORK YEARS

After Joe McCarthy notified me through a flunky that I was no longer needed, I went to New York. Here the circulation of my book in the financial capital of the world had excited much attention. I gave a number of lectures, and spent many afternoons conferring with bankers on Wall Street. I was asked to head the mutual fund department at one banking house, a development then in its infancy, but instead, I joined the American Petroleum

Institute as a consultant on taxation, where I specialized in toll road finance. After a year in this post, I was suddenly discharged the day after the new edition of my Federal Reserve book was published, in 1954. Because my employers refused to give any reason for my discharge, filed suit against them, leaving the details to my attorney. When he allowed the case to lapse, I did not reopen it, for my reason in filing the suit was to show that my record was clear, and that I was willing to go into any court to defend myself. In any case, it would have been impossible for me to win a favorable verdict in New York's Yiddish courts, which were merely side-offices of the Anti-Defamation League. I later learned that my discharge from the American Petroleum Institute had been at the personal demand of a Jew named Jacob Blaustein, president of the American Oil Company. During my researches at the Library of Congress, I had come across some court cases in which Blaustein's father figured, during several trials based on his profession of setting up dummy oil companies for Standard Oil of New York. On several occasions during these trials, Blaustein was told that because of his thick, Yiddish accent, the judge could not understand his testimony, the inference being that Blaustein was pretending to be more illiterate than he actually was.

CHICAGO YEARS

I had been in correspondence with Mrs. Lyr1 Clark Van

Hyning, the courageous publisher of Women's Voice. I admired her for the splendid work she was doing, although I did not yet know that she was the only right-wing publisher whose organization had not been infiltrated and taken over by the Anti-Defamation League, to be used by them to harass patriots and also to extort money from the Jewish community. I decided to accept her invitation to visit Chicago. We got out some terrific issues of her paper, and then I realized that my money was almost gone.

In Chicago, as in New York, I had met many wealthy and patriotic Americans who admired me, who believed in my work, and who were delighted to take me to the most expensive night clubs and restaurants in order to tell me how terrible everything was. While the smothered me with praise, I never saw as much as a ten-dollar bill from any one of them, although their personal holdings were in the millions, with one "patriot" who had a fortune of fifty million dollars, and who once treated me to a home-cooked dinner of roast beef, Here I was treading in the footsteps of foe McCarthy, who had also been wined and dined by these same millionaires. When he needed a few thousand dollars to pay his office bills, and was threatened with assassination by the Jews, he received not an iota of help from the American right wing, and was thrown to the wolves of the Anti-Defamation League, while his crusade against Communism was scuttled by Cohn and Schine.

Without assistance from anyone, I obtained the position of feature writer for Institutions Magazine, and after a few months, I was offered a much better-paying job as director of publications for the Chicago Motor Club. Thus the Institutions position turned out to be the only fob I held in my life from which the AIL and the FBI did not get me fired. After eighteen months with the Chicago Motor Club, during which I initiated four new programs in the department of public relations which were eminently successful, two FBI agents visited my employer at two p.m. one afternoon. As they went into his Ace, one of them threw me a sneering but triumphant glance. They were with him forty-five minutes. He left with them, to visit his doctor, I later learned, for he had had three heart attacks, and the FBI agents made threats against him when he balked at discharging me, so that he had to have two hypodermics before going home.

He called the office after going to his doctor, and told his secretary to inform me that I had ten minutes to get my things and leave the premises. As on previous occasions, the announcement created consternation among my fellow-workers. Two of the secretaries were in tears, because I had always treated them considerately, unlike some of my fellow executives, but I left with as little disturbance as possible. I had some savings, and was not worried about getting another job, because I had made many friends in Chicago's business community, had raised large sums for the Red Cross, and had been active in many public relations activities.

DIFFICULT YEARS

I left the Chicago Motor Club in good health, thirty-five years old, and with no immediate problems. After a few weeks, I found that I had been turned down for a half-dozen jobs which had seemed tailor-made for someone with my ability and experience. A friend on the Chicago Tribune informed me that my employer had been answering all requests for references by telephone, refusing to put anything into writing. He had told all inquirers that I was an habitual criminal with a long police record, and that I was unbalanced and considered to be quite dangerous. Although I could not obtain this in writing, I sued the Chicago Motor Club for $200,000. The case came up before a judge who was known as the Mafia's man in Chicago, and who also frequently lunched with the executives of the Motor Club. He dismissed my suit with prejudice, and some months later, when the Mafia had occasion to think he was double-crossing them, his plane was blown up over Gary, Indiana, killing him and his unlucky fellow-passengers.

SERENITY

Although it now seemed impossible that I could obtain any sort of a job in Chicago, I continued to work without pay for Mrs. Van Hyning, as did all of her supporters. Her husband paid most of the expenses. One afternoon, a well-to-do lady who helped support the paper invited us to lunch in a restaurant frequented by the City Hall politicos. It was a pleasant meal, and that evening, Mrs. Van Hyning remarked, "Mrs. was rather surprised by you. today." 'What did I do?" I asked. "She couldn't get over the fact that you were so calm," replied Mrs. Van Hyning. "She knows what you've been through lately."

In retrospect, I realized that I was calm. Although I did not know it, I was serene in the Love of Jesus Christ. Mrs. an Hyning knew it, but as usual, she kept her own counsel, leaving me to make this discovery for myself. Other people seemed surprised that I had not had a nervous breakdown, or tried to commit suicide, after having my life shattered three times within five years by AL and FBI viciousness in having me discharged from well-paying and responsible positions. The fact was that I had never once thought about it, being too busy on the new book which always faced me, and turning out the articles which had transformed right wing periodicals from AL-controlled butcher sheets filled with silly tirades against the Jews to hard-hitting and newsworthy papers which printed all the news excluded by the metropolitan press.

LIVING IN CHRIST

It was another five years before I realized that I was living in Christ. By that time, I had passed through the murder of my father, had survived a number of attempts against my life, and had settled down to living on the barest level of subsistence, without money for medical care or any of the amenities of life. Despite all this, I seemed to be becoming stronger, while friends Who, on the surface, had everything, substantial incomes, beautiful homes and families, responsible positions, seemed to be losing ground and growing more dejected each year.

Although Mrs. Van Hyping did not bring me to Christ, for no one can do that for you, it was my association with her which finally revealed to me that I was living in Christ, At no time during my years of arduous and un-rewarded activity did it occur to me that I was doing this for Christ. Like most young men of some ability, I believed that I was following my own course, for my own purposes. I was creating a reputation for myself as a writer, blazing new trails which brought me much praise and a great deal of satisfaction, and I had pitted myself against the most powerful and vicious banking and crime syndicates ever known to man.

In all this, even though I worked for little financial return, I still thought of achieving success in conventional terms, having a home and a family of my own, earning substantial annual royalties from my books, and being able to afford some of the rewards of a busy and useful life. This was not a dream, but a concept, and as the years passed, and I worked harder, and had less, it gradually receded from me. And as this material world faded from my mind, I found that I had come into a Presence, an immensely patient and calm and beautiful Radiance, until I began to realize from whence had come the patience and the calm which had brought me through these terrible years, years which no longer seemed terrible at all, but permeated with a wonderful and lingering Radiance, and then I knew that I had been allowed a reward which few men have ever known, the sublimely beautiful Presence of Jesus Christ.

REAL LIFE

As I began to know Christ, and to know myself, I began to know life, real life, not the false and hopeless existence in Satan which is the lot of most men. I was relieved from the frantic scramble for material possessions which is the Purgatory of man's life on earth. And by going beyond materialism, through knowing Christ, I began to enter the real world, and to know its possibilities, I left behind the pathetic yardsticks by which men measure each other in Satan's Empire, the yardsticks of prestige and power and success. I saw that those whom I had left in that hopeless existence were frozen in helpless and grotesque postures, which they had to maintain throughout their physical existence, and I realized the meaning of the fate of Lot, for Lot was all men who had condemned themselves to become monstrous statues in the material world, and who, while they supposed that they lived and breathed, actually passed their lives in a single frozen position. But is living in Christ an immaterial existence? It is material but it is not imprisoned in the material world, man is not a frozen statue. That is why Satan's Empire uses the Stone Age Jews and the traps of materialism to hold man back from the real world, that is why Communism, which advertised itself as "the wave of the future", has sought to reinstate the institution of slavery on a worldwide basis, and to push the world back to the prehistoric concepts of the Stone Age Jews.

The human organism needs certain elements of food, clothing and shelter, but only Satan and the Jews and the Communists claim that this is all there is to life. Christ reminds man that he has a mission, that the Self has a direction, and that if this direction is not followed, man does not have life, he does not know himself, he does not know Christ, he does not know the world.

Satan's historic allies are fear and greed, and it is these forces which deliver man into the hands of the Jews and the Communists. But living in Christ, man never again knows the fear of not having enough, while greed does not exist. Thus man is freed from the terrible daily scramble to maintain existence. Material things are reduced to their proper plane, while the higher mission of the Self is expressed. This is why Christ stated that a rich man could not enter Heaven, any more than a camel could pass through the eye of the needle. He did not say that it was wrong to be rich, He merely pointed out that the man who enters Heaven is not a rich man, because he does not bring material wealth into Heaven with him, it remains behind, in the earthly sphere. Being rich is not in itself wrong, although the rich sometimes become possessed by their wealth, they are overcome by the daemonic factor of great wealth, but the rich man can save himself from being turned into a demon by knowing Christ.

The freedom from the daily scramble for economic factors is only the first benefit in knowing Christ, it is only one aspect of attaining serenity through the Love of Jesus Christ. As one liberates the Self, one creates a whole new personality in Jesus, without sacrificing any of the personal factors of one's old life. In effect, one recovers from an illness, the sickness of living in Satan's Empire, and one becomes a healthy person. One becomes responsible for one's Self, and instead of being a burden, one is able to help others.

THE MURDER OF MY FATHER

We now come to an event of which I cannot write without tears, seven years later. This is the harassment of my father by government agents until his death, solely because he was my father. The FBI was given orders to carry out this mission for only one reason — they had been unable to locate any source of financial support for me, and they concluded that any father must be underwriting my activities. A cursory examination of his finances would have shown that this was impossible —

he lived very modestly on a very modest salary. Nevertheless, I was continuing to study, travel, write, and lecture on the crime of Communist subversion in America, and the orders were that something must be done. A left-wing writer, working for Communism, would have functioned on a personal budget of from fifty to one hundred thousand dollars a year, supplied by such groups as the Carnegie Foundation (Alger Hiss or the Rockefeller Foundation (Dean Rusk), in order to achieve the sheer volume of my output.

I had transformed the anti-Communist press from a loose network of ineffectual, ADL-controlled organs to a hard-hitting group of papers publishing well-documented articles, and which were having a tremendous impact all over America. Much of my material had appeared in the Congressional record, and was quoted elsewhere. For more than a decade, my articles and books had begun to build a solid, well-informed, anti-Communist underground in America to combat the government of the anti-Christ in Washington. Not one statement which appeared under my name had eyer been challenged — not one charge of any kind had ever been brought against me, although I had never hesitated to sue the Communist press for libelling me, nor feared to stand on my record anywhere. I had also voluntarily appeared to defend patriots who had been charged with crimes after the FBI had planted evidence against them, In every case in which I had appeared, the intended victims had been freed. The FBI directorate bitterly hated me for this record of defeating them.

My father had never been in a court room in his life, nor had he ever been charged with any offence. Insofar as I know, he had never in his life received anything which he had not earned by his own labour, nor had be ever asked for anything. He had worked continuously since the age of twelve, and at the age of sixty, he had had one three-day vacation in his life, an automobile trip to Washington, D. C.

MURDER, INC.

Every American knows that Lyndon Baines Johnson became President of the United States because of the murder of John F. Kennedy. But few Americans know that he had become Vice-President, in a position to shoot for the Presidency, because he acquiesced in the murder of my father.

Lyndon Baines Johnson appeared in swirling clouds of evil, seething mists of sex perversion, unsolved murders and overnight fortunes. He also inherited Franklin D. Roosevelt's sinister crew of Communist Jews in Washington, and he became their abject slave. His close friend, Senator Herbert Lehman, who had demanded that I be discharged from the Library of Congress, was dismayed that the Anti-Defamation League of B'nai B'rith, which he headed, had been unable to halt my crusade against Communism. Now Lehman decided that my family must be attacked until I gave in, to protect them, and ceased my work for Christ.

Lehman asked the then Senator Johnson to help him get Army Counter-Intelligence Corps credentials for two agents of the Israeli Army, Johnson agreed, and these two agents visited my father, made many threats against him, and as a warning, gave him a severe beating. A few hours later, he suffered a severe coronary attack from which he never completely recovered.

Some months later, the FBI employed one of their most depraved and trusted minions in New Jersey to deliver the final blow against my father. This creature, a notorious sex deviate, had, some years earlier, been charged with molesting children, and had been sentenced to a. ten-thousand-dollar fine and a six months jail term. The FBI then informed him that the sentence would be suspended indefinitely if he carried out some minor chores for them. During the next several years, these duties involved spying on anti-Communist organizations, procuring boys for the pleasure of highly placed government deviates in Washington, and rifling the apartments of persons in whom the FBI had an interest.

Johnson had already been given his reward, the Vice-Presidential nomination, with Kennedy. This nomination stunned everyone in the political know, because it was as unlikely a twosome as Eisenhower and Heinrich

Himmler. The pundits confessed that they were mystified by this choice, because they did not know that Herbert Lehman, one of the world's most powerful international Jewish bankers and a consistent apologist for world Communism, had ordered John F. Kennedy to accept Johnson, as a reward for his participation in the brutal assault upon my father.

When Herbert Lehman died, President Johnson dropped everything and rushed to New York to attend his funeral. As he entered the synagogue, Johnson was heard to murmur reverentially, "He was one of the great ones. He opened many doors for me."

Although Lehman had played no part in the assassination of Kennedy, he had made it all possible by thrusting an eager Johnson upon the unwilling and rather bitter Kennedys.

THE ASSASSIN'S BLOW

Now the FBI ordered the deviate to place a long-distance call to my father, informing him that the FBI had issued a national alert for me, and that I was to be arrested on sight, and killed if I resisted. Because the deviate had once visited my home on the pretence of asking me to write an article for a letterhead group which he and the FBI used to mislead patriots, my father had met him, and knew nothing against him. The deviate pretended, in making this call, that he wished to help me, and to have my family alert me against the expected arrest and imprisonment. My father had never recovered from the heart attack brought on by the beating administered to him by the agents of the Israeli Army, and I believe that he had been subjected to a great deal of further harassment which he never mentioned to anyone. At any rate, his health was precarious, and after talking to the deviate, he turned to my mother and said, "This is it. They've finally got Clarence." Then he collapsed.

He died some hours later in a local hospital, the verdict being hypertension. At this time, I had been residing quietly in an apartment near New York for some months, working on a revision of my Federal Reserve book. My name was in the telephone book, the lights and water were in my name, and of course the FBI had been keeping my apartment under the usual observation.

There was no national alert for me, I had not then or at any time since been charged with any offence, but the FBI had achieved their objective. My father was dead.

ATTEMPTS AGAINST MY LIFE

I had already survived a number of attempts against my life, which had begun shortly after I sued the Chicago Motor Club. I had known that the Motor Club was principally owned by the Mafia, but I had not realized that they would issue a contract for my murder simply because I had filed suit against them. However, I received a telephoned warning from a former fellow- editor, and was on my guard when the first attempt came. After two such attempts, I left Chicago and went to New York, where other attempts were made.

AT HOME IN VIRGINIA

When I returned to Virginia for my father's funeral, the first night I was home, the police ticketed my car for not having a local license. Although the charge was dismissed, this was the first instance of a steady police harassment, to let me know that I was not welcome there. George Sokolsky wrote a series of columns, denouncing me as a "fascist" and a "subversive" because I had defended the United States Constitution, and because I had called attention to Sokolsky's sinister activities in Russia during the Bolshevik Revolution. The local newspaper ran the columns, and refused to print a retraction, so I filed suit against them, but my attorney kept postponing the case, and was later disbarred for forgery. In the meantime, he had let the suit lapse and it was dismissed.

I remained at home, to care for my mother, whose health was precarious, and it was more than a year later before she dared to tell me the circumstances of my father's death. Despite my tremendous anger, there was nothing I could do, because the deviate was still under the official protection of the FBI. I continued to be on my guard, but I finally realized that there would be no attempts on my life while I remained in Virginia. The reason was that I was now protected by the Byrd machine, and this also was a long story.

THE CRIME AGAINST MY SISTER

When my sister was two years old, she had been crushed beneath the wheels of a hit and run driver. The driver was identified by a number of witnesses as a local real estate magnate, H. H. Marklev, who was also a power in the Democratic state machine, He kept a suite of rooms in the Ponce de Leon Hotel, in which nude girls served whiskey to the politicians. In exchange, Markley had received many favours from the Byrd Machine.

Now a local fudge, a close friend of Markley, beard the case and intimidated my parents into settling for partial payment of my sister's hospital bills, even though she had been crippled for life. Not only had her speech been affected, but the central nerve in her neck had been crushed, causing her to become mentally retarded. The judge went on to become a Governor of Virginia, and my parents were faced with the problem of caring for my sister for the rest of her life.

I had made some efforts to reopen the case, but I had found that all court records had mysteriously disappeared, as had my sister's hospital records at the University of Virginia. The fact that I had done this now proved to be a protection for me. The Byrd politicians did not wish anything to happen to me while I remained in Virginia, because this would focus new attention upon my sister s unfortunate history. As a result, I could start my car without lifting the hood, or looking in the back seat to see who might be hidden there.

The Byrd machine itself had made Virginia a travesty of the Cradle of Democracy which had been its previous reputation. A Virginia President, Woodrow Wilson, had enslaved Americans with the income tax, whose successful passage in 1913 had been largely due to the assistance given Wilson by Senator Carter Glass, who later became senile in office and became a tragic joke as a representative of the people.

Harry Byrd tightened the reins until every office in the State of Virginia was held by faceless time-servers who were completely subservient to him, while he was completely subservient to Jewish bankers in New York. His affairs were handled by Lewis Lichtenstein Strauss, a partner of Kuhn, Loebe Co., who made all of his investments for him. When Bernard Baruch wanted a Senator to ramrod through the confirmation of the left-wing Anna Rosenberg, his former secretary, as Assistant Secretary of Defence, he made a personal call to Harry Byrd. Anna Rosenberg was confirmed.

This, then, was the strange crew to which I now owed my freedom from further attacks against my life. As usual, I made use of the opportunity, continuing to turn out my work, completing my definitive work, The History of the Jews, and laying the outlines of other books.

THE ARMY OF CHRIST

In continuing my work, and in living in Christ, I had become a member of the Army of Christ. Now, even though one lives in Christ, one is still living in a world at war, a war torn by the struggle between good and evil, Christ's effort to overthrow Satan's Empire by creating a revolution in the soul of man. This meant that the Radiance of Christ must overcome and transform man, lift him up from the terrible inertia to which Satan has condemned him, and bring him out into the real world.

Being in the Army of Christ means duty, work and discipline. It means not swerving from the objective, carrying out one's assignments, and refusing to be misled by those wearing the correct uniform but who are really in the service of the enemy. None of this is difficult for one who apprises himself of the Pure Nature of Christ, because that Purity informs everything on earth, and identifies everything as black or white, for Christ or for Satan.

CHRIST POWER

Many people have asked me, "How is it that you have been able to accomplish so much in your life, when you have no money, no power, and no influence? How have you managed to write your books, study, travel, and lecture on the dangers of Communism and Satan's Empire on earth?"

It is true that I have had no money and no power, but I do not want money and power in Satan's world. And I have had some influence. I have known many of the wealthiest and most powerful men in America, but these people were not able to help me in the work, because they had become frozen in their roles, they had suffered the fate of Lot and had been turned into pillars of salt because they looked back, they were not able to look ahead.

The problem was not that they were unable or unwilling to help me, but that I had not been able to help them, because I had not progressed far enough in Christ. These wealthy and powerful men needed my help! I needed nothing from them, but at this stage of my development, I was unable to help them because I had not yet mastered the secret of Christ Power. Now I can reveal this secret to the world.

The secret of Christ Power lies in the nature of human potential. The human potential can only be realized if it is released and directed, and this means that it must find a goal outside of the individual and in another sphere. Now, one avenue of this release of the human potential is through Satan. Those who give themselves to Satan suddenly have avenues of earthly wealth and power opened to them, but they have no idea that this is only a small fraction of their true potential. The potential which we can realize through Satan is quite limited, otherwise Satan would have attained a complete victory eons ago.

The other avenue of release of human potential is through Christ, and this release is, as we know potential, unlimited from our limited point of view. That is, the things which we can accomplish are so vast that we cannot even imagine them in our present state.

Christ Power is not an esoteric thing, it is a law of physics. How does it work? Only in this more modern age can we begin to understand it, through our advance in knowledge of planets and space, and other phenomena of physics. The human potential is a form of energy, essentially a radiance. Now, in Christ Power, we direct our radiance to Christ, and it is returned to us magnified a hundredfold. This is the beginning of the process, as the radiance is beamed back and forth between us and Christ in an accelerating ratio. It is magnified each time, but slowly and carefully, otherwise the sudden increase in our energy would destroy us and we would vanish in an instant. This is why people must spend years in the work before being led into the Way, as Christ gradually allows us to increase our human potential, our radiance which is only a pale and infinitesimal glow of His Radiance.

EDUCATION IN CHRIST

Because of the years of training which are required if we are to realize anything of our potential, we can see that most of our "education", our formal schooling, is wasted. I stunned the academic world in 1955 with an article in Women's Voice, "Close the Public Schools!"

The article was sound and well-reasoned, for public education was less than a century old, and it was demonstrably a dismal failure in every value judgment. Ten years later, quite respectable educators began to suggest that the public-school system in America was beyond salvaging, and that it might be wiser to return to a system of private schools.

We refuse to acknowledge that the public-school system has already collapsed. Teacher strikes, classrooms which are jungles, and student riots, have paralysed the educational process. From student riots at Berkeley to the play schools of elementary education, the system is a farce maintained by educators only to hold on to their influential and well-paying jobs.

What is education? Education means "being led into knowledge". A child should be led only in a sacred context, it must be education in Christ. Why is this? Children are beautiful in our eves because they are fresh sources of energy, their radiance is undimmed. But this radiance is soon destroyed through the futility of public education.

Men and women age because their radiance is not used, it has no opportunity to go out of the individual and to grow in Christ. Some day, humans will learn to use and to thrive upon their radiance, and they will be beautiful throughout their lives, while life will be quite unlike life as we know it now.

When I say "education in Christ", of course I do not refer to present day "religious" education. Learning to use one's radiance and to live with Christ Power has no relation to learning how many saints can dance on the head of a pin. Without Christ, man always sinks to the lowest common denominator, to the animal level of Stone Age Jews. In the public schools, which mingle children from all walks of life, they quickly sink to the lowest common denominator. The private schools, which are more rigorous in their admissions policies, are vastly superior because of this one difference, and because their education often is placed in a religious atmosphere. But even the finest private schools are nothing to what they will become if they inaugurate a system of education in Christ. Now, what does this mean? It means that the child will realize that his chance to grow, which is all that education can offer, would take place under the most favourable auspices, in the Love and Radiance of Christ.

Eustace Mullins   Ezra Pound who was influential in setting Eustace on a lifelong mission to expose corruption in high places.

Eustace Mullins still working at 84

"For out of Zion shall go forth the law,
and the Word of the Lord from Jerusalem" **(Isaiah 2:3)**."

Other work by Eustace Mullins

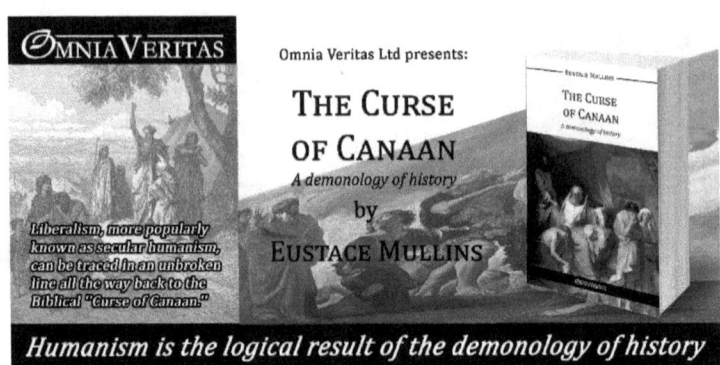

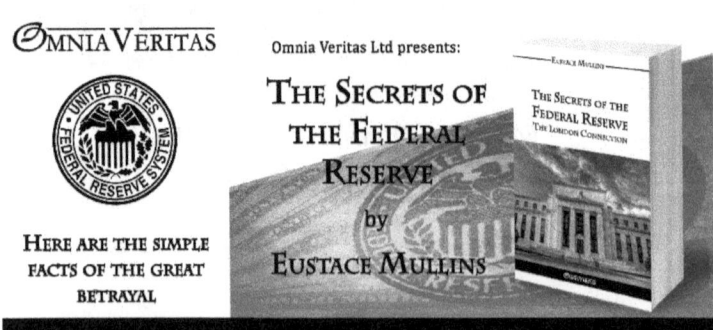

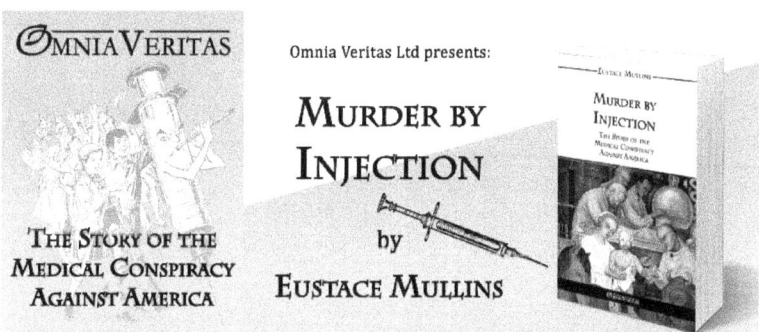
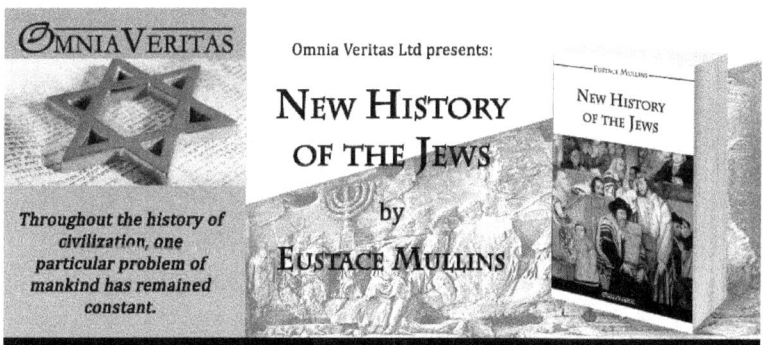

www.ingramcontent.com/pod-product-compliance
Lightning Source LLC
Chambersburg PA
CBHW070918160426
43193CB00011B/1511